T0397128

"Amy Heusterberg-Richards's *All Subjects in Play* redefines secondary education through play-based learning. Her innovative strategies enhance student engagement and foster critical thinking. This book is a must-read for educators looking to inspire and connect with their students."

Damian LaCroix, *Wisconsin State Superintendent of the Year*

"As someone who has long championed the importance of play and physical activity in K-8 classrooms, I am thrilled to see Amy Heusterberg-Richards focus on extending these vital practices to the secondary level in *All Subjects in Play*. Her insightful approach highlights the critical role of play in fostering creativity, collaboration, and deeper learning for older students. This book is a must-read for educators looking to energize their classrooms and reimagine how play can transform student engagement and success."

Dr. Brad Johnson, *Speaker, Author of* Dear Teacher: 100 Days of Inspirational Quotes and Anecdotes

All Subjects in Play

Even older students can benefit from play in the classroom—and it doesn't mean sacrificing rigor. Seasoned educator Amy Heusterberg-Richards shows teachers how embracing play in secondary classrooms can build content, refine skills, and assess understanding, all while inviting joy back into the classrooms of teens who often feel anxious and disfranchised about education.

This book describes approaches and rationale for embedding play within secondary classrooms across all disciplines. Each of the 20 lessons includes research-based rationales, step-by-step instructions, samples, student-facing directions, and applications across subject areas. Artificial intelligence (AI)-incorporated ideas are also provided. In a world with apathy and AI, education—even at the secondary level—needs to embrace the ever-natural, always-cathartic experience of playing.

By thoughtfully integrating play-based learning, we can enhance classroom management, maintain academic standards, cover the curriculum effectively, and engage older students in meaningful ways. High school learners, too, can laugh and create and pretend as they learn.

Amy Heusterberg-Richards holds 18 years of high school English Language Arts teaching experience and is a decade-long International Baccalaureate teacher. In 2018, she was Wisconsin's selectee and national qualifier for the NCTE Teacher of Excellence title. She has presented at several conferences and has been published on Moving Writers and Edutopia. Her Twitter/X handle is @LAwithMrsHR.

Also Available from Routledge Eye on Education
www.routledge.com/k-12

**Joyful Learning: Tools to Infuse Your 6-12 Classroom
with Meaning, Relevance, and Fun**
Stephanie Farley

**The Heart-Centered Teacher: Restoring Hope, Joy,
and Possibility in Uncertain Times**
Regie Routman

**The Student Motivation Handbook: 50 Ways to Boost
an Intrinsic Desire to Learn**
Larry Ferlazzo

**Working Hard, Working Happy: Cultivating a Culture
of Effort and Joy in the Classroom**
Rita Platt

Motivating Struggling Learners: 10 Ways to Build Student Success
Barbara R. Blackburn

All Subjects in Play

Play-Based Lessons for the Secondary Classroom

Amy Heusterberg-Richards

Routledge
Taylor & Francis Group

NEW YORK AND LONDON

Designed cover image: Getty Images

First published 2025
by Routledge
605 Third Avenue, New York, NY 10158

and by Routledge
4 Park Square, Milton Park, Abingdon, Oxon, OX14 4RN

Routledge is an imprint of the Taylor & Francis Group, an informa business

ISBN: 978-1-032-97054-7 (hbk)
ISBN: 978-1-032-97048-6 (pbk)
ISBN: 978-1-003-59192-4 (ebk)

DOI: 10.4324/9781003591924

Typeset in Palatino
by codeMantra

Access the Support Material: www.routledge.com/9781032970486

Contents

Support Material

The Escape Room handouts are also available as free downloads in full color on our website, so you can easily download and print them for classroom use. To access the materials, go to the book product page at routledge.com/9781032970486 and click the link that says Support Material.

Meet the Author

Amy Heusterberg-Richards is a dedicated mom, proud wife, and engaged educator in Green Bay, Wisconsin, who currently teaches high school English Language Arts just north of Lambeau Field's frozen tundra. She holds a BA in English, Spanish, and Secondary Education from St. Norbert College; earned an MA in Applied Teaching and Learning from the University of Wisconsin-Green Bay; and was selected as Wisconsin's 2018 NCTE Teacher of Excellence. In her free time, Amy enjoys gardening, coffee, reading, and family time.

1

Introduction

My first airplane ride was from my cold, Wisconsin hometown to the warm, sun-dressed beaches of Florida. While our trip to Disney World is stored somewhere in my mind, the memory that strikes me most from this vacation is one moment of jumping over waves in the ocean with my late father. Feeling encouraged by the strong presence of an adult, I held my dad's hands as both he and the waves lifted me up with each passing movement. I bobbed up and down, supported by his safety and invigorated by the newness of the ocean experience.

And while I had to take a plane to arrive at the Atlantic, in my day-to-day childhood I was no stranger to the ever-wondrous experience of large bodies of water. A car ride of mere minutes east and I could stand on the shores of Lake Michigan, one of the largest freshwater lakes in the world. Lake Michigan, like that Floridian sea, swarms with white-capped waves—ones that on a stormy day can encapsulate even the tallest midwestern lighthouses.

Those of us in education know that our field, not unlike others, is also dotted by waves. In my two decades as a teacher, I can recall the flipped learning wave, the blended learning wave, the personalized learning wave, and so many others. Now as I write in 2024, educators are wading cautiously into the seeming tsunami of artificial intelligence's (AI) presence in schools. No opponent of change, I've used at least four different digital learning management systems and speckled my room with desks and then roundtables and then exercise balls and then soft furniture and then chairs again.

DOI: 10.4324/9781003591924-1

Like my vacation waves of Florida and hometown waves of Lake Michigan, such educational movements can arrive with fervor. They sweep teachers away with passion. They wash through interviews as question focuses and answer buzzwords. They flood classrooms with trials and budgets with purchases.

Throughout most of my youth, though, there were no waves to lift and release me as I swam on summer weekday afternoons in my own backyard. Wisconsin's freezing winter temperatures are juxtaposed with equally fierce summer weather, so my family had a small above-ground pool to cool off in those hot months. Without waves to determine my movement—within those *ordinary* waters, I would dive for colorful sticks, float on silly tubes, and play games with neighbor children.

No one taught me how to splash and giggle in the pool. No outside current directed my movement. And no one needed to hold my hand as I swam in that familiar, wave-less space.

My pool games were natural—the play itself, as for all children: instinctive.

Now, as a parent myself, I see similar splashes and hear familiar giggles when I venture to our neighborhood pool with my two children and their friends. Decades and technologies later, kids still gleefully swim with dive sticks and roll off inflatable tubes.

Despite educational waves, pool play is still simply and wonderfully pool play.

Conversely, despite AI's tsunamic emergence, video-game play is also still video-game play. With a tweenage son, I'm well aware that "artificial" actors have been present in the gaming world for many, many years now. NPCs (non-player characters) are game avatars with whom real human gamers interact but who exist as artificial characters. The video gaming world has not become replaced by sophisticated NPCs, though, because the act of video gaming continues to attract human players.

Play. That's the instinctive action in the pool and the continual verb in the "cheat"-potential gaming world.

Play remains constant throughout waves and with technologies.

Play is active, it is challenging, it propels growth, and it incites passion.

In an educational system strategizing its own NPC-esque experience with AI, let's refocus on the natural, human experience of play. In a 21st century that fears screen-obsessed teens, let's lean into playful learning approaches for secondary students. In a nation confronting ever-rising concerns about anxieties in young people and behaviors in schools, let's prompt the laughter of children at play.

2

This Book's Aims

In this book, I offer strategies and rationale for embedding play within secondary classrooms and across subject-matter disciplines. Because educators value knowledge as much as they adore children, each lesson description begins with research that supports the approach. The book explores the "what does that look like" and "what steps do I take" of purposeful, play-based learning for older students. Purposeful, in this case, means the play presented does not surround getting to know learners—like icebreaker games—or exist to "fill in extra time," as in nonacademic work. While such activities are wonderful in building connected and comfortable classrooms, the academic play presented here seeks to build content, refine skills, and assess understanding.

While incredible resources are emerging about incorporating play into primary classrooms and as entire elementary schools, tween/teen learners are generally under considered. I anticipate some educators still feel skeptical about marrying play-based learning with advanced studies. There are likely experienced teachers of adolescents out there reading this introduction and thinking:

> My freshman learners have a hard enough time using their pencils appropriately. You know what kind of ridiculous shapes I'm going to see if I give them play-doh?! Secondary-level classroom management is hard enough as it is. I need a serious classroom, not a silly one.

DOI: 10.4324/9781003591924-2

And, I'd be dishonest if I claimed to never have had a pencil thrown in my ceiling tiles or a phallic doodle found somewhere throughout my classroom. Last school year, I brought small pumpkins into school for my seniors to decorate with analytical claims and textual evidence. Some of my sophomore students, unbeknownst to me, added anatomical graffiti to the Lit-o-Lanterns later that day, too. (See the "Additional Child's Play for Content-Building" for pictures of doodle-free pumpkins.) It's understandable to worry about classroom management challenges—especially as navigating such seems to get increasingly harder year after year.

Educators know, though, that off-task behaviors most often happen when structure is low, expectations are unclear, and engagement is one-sided. Integrating play-based learning in secondary classrooms can be done with clarity and be used for productivity. Furthermore, teachers who encourage play do not need to sacrifice control. They will, though, propel student creativity. Play—when paired with well-defined goals and expectations—can actually help maintain a focused and respectful classroom environment.

> *I lecture well, and my students are off to college soon—where they'll have to sit and listen. Play has no place in advanced studies. We need to encourage rigor in academic environments in order to prepare students for the "real world."*

Correct. Some collegiate studies do employ more traditional methods of instruction, like expert lectures and Socratic seminars. These approaches hold value, too, and I will not use this book to dismiss ideas like Project Follow Through's praise of direct instruction or the centuries-tried successes of dialogic discussions. Instead, I'd prefer to offer a "yes, and…" to note that creative thinking and problem-solving will also be needed for the "real world." My two children, unfortunately, will need to be prepared to tackle issues like political polarization, climate change, resource scarcity, economic inequality, environmental degradation, and more. At its core, play is solving problems and displaying creativity—with encouraged independence and hopeful joy.

I also cannot argue that rigor and joy need to be separate experiences. Modern colleges and workplaces know such, too, and are including playful spaces in their professional environments. Acuity, a local-to-me insurance company that consistently and nationally ranks as an ideal employer contains a symbolic Ferris wheel in its headquarters' center. Google is famous for encouraging slides over stairs (Google's Office Slides 2012), and Facebook headquarters playfully includes a graffiti wall for workers and visitors (Edelhauser 2007). Our students' workplaces will not be those of our parents; instead, companies are learning that encouraging play through game rooms and the like encourages employee satisfaction, productivity, and collaboration.

My state/district/school requires me to get through so much educational material already. Adding "play" is only going to slow me down when I have high school-level assessments, like the ACT and AP/IB exams, for which to prepare.

Incorporating play-based learning does not necessarily mean slowing down curriculum. As the research presented throughout the approach-focused sections of this book suggests, play-based teaching actually enhances retention and critical thought. When students are actively engaged and enjoy what they are learning, they grasp complex material quickly and thoroughly. Additionally, many of the tried-and-true play-based approaches I offer here are strategies that have been employed in a college-credit course of twelfth graders. This course attracts academically top-performing learners and, ultimately, a decade of students have had great success on their college-credit exams.

Fine, but real talk: There's no way I can get my seventeen- and eighteen-year-old learners to engage in "childish" games. Plus, I'd feel awkward and unprepared asking them to play.

What is teaching but being awkward in front of a classroom of teenagers? ☺

But, really, this reservation highlights a feeling that I've had with various "suggested" classroom activities throughout my career, too. In truth, any teaching/learning approach that does not honor the ability and maturity levels of students can create an uncomfortable experience for everyone involved. Hopefully, the age-appropriate and relevant design of these playful approaches will remedy any potential discomfort. And, instead of mere "childish games," this book will present research-based challenges, simulations, role-playing, creativity prompts, and gamified experiences. Even high school seniors can be more engaged and motivated when learning activities are presented in a playful format that requires strategic thinking and collaboration.

Okay, be silly if you'd like, but isn't "play" an outdated approach? Shouldn't we be focusing on technology, especially in an AI-introduced world?

If your classroom is at all like mine, cell phone (mis)use is a significant and central obstacle in teaching, learning, and the overall well-being of your students. If your school is similar to mine, artificial intelligence (AI) is a topic stirring conversation in most faculty meetings. Study after study provides the now-common knowledge that our technology-focused youth are more anxious, depressed, and disconnected than other generational peers. While play can be facilitated online or off, what is always needed in the act is a feeling of joy, of independence, of lightheartedness. As students navigate these mental health needs—and as they navigate those AI boundaries in a technology-obsessed world, we can support and engage them best by returning to the "natural germination" of childhood.

In a world with apathy and AI, education—even at the secondary level—needs to return to play. By thoughtfully integrating play-based learning, we can enhance classroom management, maintain academic standards, cover the curriculum effectively, and engage older students in meaningful ways.

It is entirely possible to maintain the rigor of high school while adding play-based pedagogy.

References

Edelhauser, K. "Video Games at Work?" *Entrepreneur*, Entrepreneur Media, LLC, 4 June 2007, https://www.entrepreneur.com/growing-a-business/video-games-at-work-entrepreneurcom/179274.

"Google's Office Slides." *Business Insider*, 14 May 2012, https://www.businessinsider.com/googles-office-slides-2012-5.

3

This Book's Structure

I've structured the book's contents into three sections, just as a secondary educator might organize an instructional unit:

1. The first section offers no/low-prep lessons to use play to build content understanding.
2. The second section—admittedly consisting of my favorite lessons—presents strategies to use play-based learning as a means to apply and extend students' skills.
3. The third section, like the end of a unit, offers a play-based summative assessment approach.

Within each section, you'll find:

- ◆ Research on the approach's rationale.
- ◆ Step-by-step explanations of how to play.
- ◆ Samples of each play approach.
- ◆ Student-facing instructions to replicate.
- ◆ Application of the play across secondary subjects.

Additionally, an artificial intelligence (AI)-included idea completes both lesson sections to model how this new technology (as it exists in 2024 while I'm writing) might support play in secondary classrooms. Despite AI's challenges, I strongly believe that educators should embrace changing times and that emerging technology can, in fact, enhance learners' instinct to play.

DOI: 10.4324/9781003591924-3

4

Quick Background on Play

Wherever there have been children, there has been play.

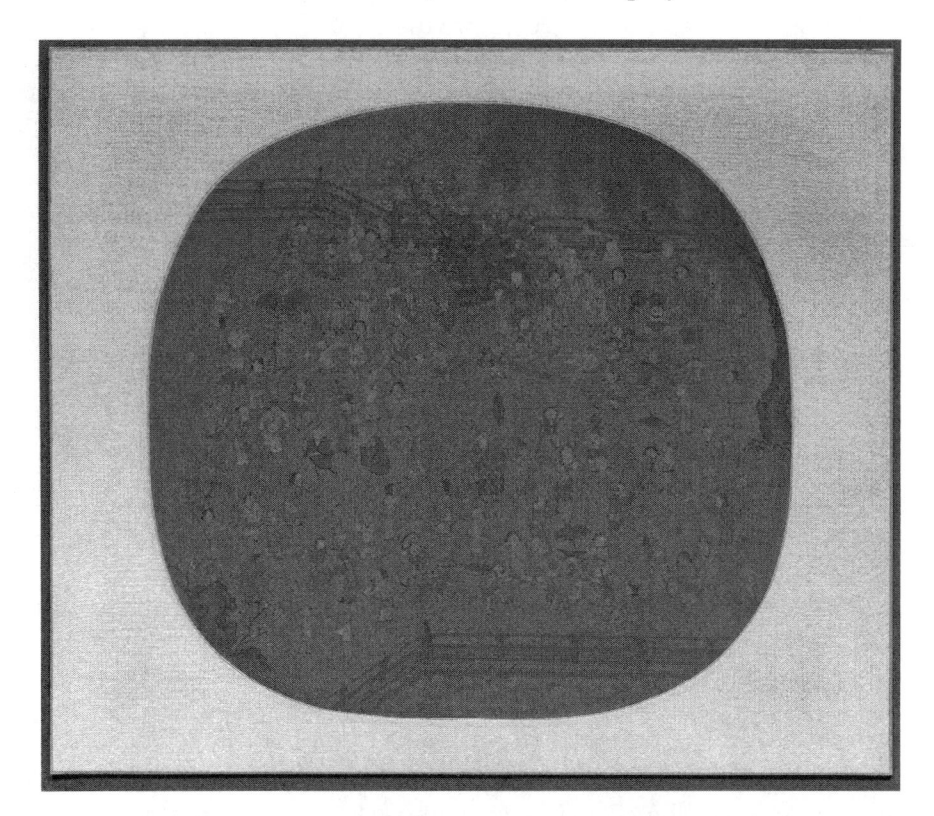

Figure 4.1 "One Hundred Children at Play" from China, Southern Song dynasty (1127–1279).

DOI: 10.4324/9781003591924-4

In societies of yore—those in which some/all children were not forced to labor, at least—like the Southern Song dynasty depicted in Figure 4.1, children ran (Su and Wang 1101). And laughed. And made music. They engaged in dramatic role-playing. In ancient Greece, young people would use bones and bladders from pigs to create ball games (7 Ways Children Used to Play Throughout History 2024). Mancala, a wooden board on which individuals can play with seeds, beans, stones, or glass is generally believed to be the world's oldest game—dating as far back as 5800 BC in Jordan (Mancala 2020).

At the turn of modern society, early educational theorists like Johann Heinrich, Friedrich Froebel, and Maria Montessori knew that play was innate within learners and attempted to design learning through/within both structured and free play. Frobel, the German father of the kindergarten approach, perhaps best defined "play" when describing it as "the natural unfolding of the germinal leaves of childhood" (Saracho and Spodek 1995). Frobel noted that play organically occurs as children manipulate objects, craft creations, and expressively sing.

That is, through play, humanity contains the earliest germination of responsible builders, artists, and communicators.

Twentieth-century theorists continued asserting the social and psychological value of play in the lives of young children: Groos considered experimental play a child's means to "try on" adulthood. Freud used play as a therapy in which children could naturally communicate current worries and past traumas. Piaget posited stages of play, through which children progress as they develop into concrete operators. Vygotsky observed play's ability to support young people's abstract thinking, and so forth.

Today, the "right to play" is a UN-declared human right for children, with the Convention on the Rights of the Child affirming:

> *States Parties recognize the right of the child to rest and leisure, to engage in play and recreational activities appropriate to the age of the child and to participate freely in cultural life and the arts. (Article 31)*
> (Convention on the Rights of the Child 1989)

In our world that survived the COVID-19 pandemic—one in which many schools closed for the safety of their communities—more and more families are opting to homeschool or, less structured yet, "unschool" their children. Guided by the ideas of philosopher Jean-Jacques Rousseau and "fathered" by educational theorist John Holt, unschooling seeks to "keep alive the spark of curiosity and the natural love of learning with which all children are born… to accept learning as a natural part of living, and an ongoing process that continues throughout life" (Family Unschoolers Network 2006). In my own words, unschooling encourages learner play over curriculum control. As educator-experts, we know there are complexities to this apparent dismissal of the teacher's role in learning. I'd argue that "sage on the stage" and "guide on the side" are oversimplified dichotomies that diminish the pedagogical mastery knowledge of educators. And yet, traditional schools are losing students to the unschooling approach in growing waves. Perhaps teachers can implement such playful approaches for an effective balance that we in education know to be best.

When pursuing such an implementation, a quick Google of "play" and "education" renders many, many results of theories and approaches to use with *young* learners. Harvard's *A Pedagogy of Play* is an especially strong resource—one full of research and samples from elementary and middle school classrooms. The National Museum of Play, located in Rochester, New York, serves as a physical gem of play exhibits and houses a digital trove of supporting philosophies. The Lego foundation has paired with Edutopia to house *Making Learning More Playful* articles.

These play-based learning resources found today, though, focus on building experiences in the *early* education classroom.

Let's invite our biggest "kids" to the play table. Let's extend play-based learning to include our secondary learners, too.

References

"7 Ways Children Used to Play Throughout History." *Sudeley Castle*, 2024, https://sudeleycastle.co.uk/news/7-ways-children-used-to-play-throughout-history.

"Convention on the Rights of the Child." *OHCHR*, 20 Nov 1989, https://www.ohchr.org/en/instruments-mechanisms/instruments/convention-rights-child.

Family Unschoolers Network - Unschooling Support, 2006, https://www.unschooling.org/.

"Mancala." *Savannah African Art Museum*. Savannah African Art Museum, 2020.

Saracho, O. N. & Spodek, B. Children's Play and Early Childhood Education: Insights from History and Theory. *J Educ* 177(3), 129–148 (1995). *JSTOR*, https://www.jstor.org/stable/42742374.

Su, H. & Wang, J. "One Hundred Children at Play." *Cleveland Museum of Art Juzhen*, 1101, https://www.clevelandart.org/art/1961.261.

Section I

Play for Content Building

As educators know, providing students with well-built foundations of content knowledge first propels advanced skill accumulation later. Decades of research confirm—especially in core areas like reading, social studies, and science—that key content knowledge initially is pivotal for strong critical thinking next (Smith et al. 2021).

Oftentimes secondary educators use introductory readings, teacher lectures, and term recall (flashcards, etc.) to assist students in storing important, foundational content like vocabulary, dates, definitions, and so forth. Dr. Karyn Purvis, a late developmental psychologist who is especially renowned within the homeschooling world, posits: "Scientists have determined that it takes approximately 400 repetitions to create a new synapse in the brain—unless it is done with play, in which case it takes between 10-20 repetitions" (Fogg and Danyow 2023).

Using playful approaches while content-building not only creates a joyful, engaging environment with learners, but can also save time. Play-based educators who effectively build a foundation of knowledge within their subject areas can then spend more time applying related skills and guiding critical thinking.

Here are some low-prep, content-building lessons to play in your secondary classroom.

DOI: 10.4324/9781003591924-5

References

Fogg, C. & Danyow, C. "The Power of Multi-age Play-Based Learning." *Addison Independent*, 6 April 2023, https://www.addisonindependent. com/2023/04/06/the-power-of-multi-age-play-based-learning/.

Smith, R., Snow, P., Serry, T., & Hammond, L. The Role of Background Knowledge in Reading Comprehension: A Critical Review. *Reading Psychology* 42(2), 1–27 (2021).

5

"Loose Parts" Play

Projected on the instructional board, a prompt asks learners to show their growing knowledge about the structure of human cells. Spread across an empty lab table are shoeboxes of assorted items: wrapping paper scraps, half-tangled skeins of yarn, buttons inherited from an aunt, beads gathered from an outgrown craft set, and more. At each table-spot, learners begin with a sheet of construction paper, on which to build their knowledge. They chatter quietly, some glancing at their notebooks to reread the notes from earlier this week. One learner cuts a piece of yarn and creates a circle on her paper, thinking to herself that she'll depict this string as the "cell membrane" and then move to inner pieces. Another student notices the wrapping paper is festively covered with polka-dots.

"I'll cut a circle just larger than that dot," he thinks. "Then the wrapping paper can be both the nucleolus and the nucleus." Before leaving the supply table, he gathers a few beads and buttons—to represent lysosomes and ribosomes respectively.

Rationale

Pairing tangible objects with learning concepts is traditionally most common in elementary schools and, specifically, within the math field. Educators Dr. Julie P. Jones and Margaret Tiller support such play with the insight that children understand best when they can conversely see and touch, allowing concrete items like beans, cubes, chips, etc., to demonstrate thinking (Jones

DOI: 10.4324/9781003591924-6

and Southern Early Childhood Association 2017). Parents and educators alike know the excited look on a young child's face that accompanies the epiphany of a sum when fingers or spare items are involved. Interestingly, a 2016 article from the Catholic University College of Ghana suggests that even high school students studying algebra perform significantly better when using tiles as manipulatives (Larbi and Mavis 2016). With a focus on writing instruction, author and consultant Angela Stockman additionally shares how the intangible process of composing can be made known to students through physical "maker" items, like those found in nature (Stockman 2014). Regardless of discipline, experts tell us that when students can physically interact with abstract concepts, the material becomes more accessible and, conversely, memorable. By transforming abstract concepts into physical forms, students not only grasp material better but also develop more joyful and creative approaches to learning. All such research offers clear rationale: "playing" with manipulatives works.

How to Play

Known to me through my daughter's creation of a "fairy garden" in our backyard, "loose parts" is a general moniker for random and assorted items. In her fairy garden, these items tend to be shiny and/or nature-themed. In your play-encouraged classroom, they could consist of concrete items like:

- Pipe cleaners
- Pompons
- Beads/buttons
- Wooden letters
- Small cups
- Paper plates
- String
- Magazine cutouts
- Popsicle sticks
- Lego pieces

The back shelf of my classroom holds small tubs of such loose parts, to be used as needed and without preplanning. Most have been curated from craft sales and dollar racks. While I make an attempt to keep the tubs labeled, their contents generally switch as supplies come and go, as treasures are found and used.

Figure 5.1 Students use straws, cups, clothespins, pipe cleaners, coffee filters, and foil as loose parts.

While building content knowledge within your secondary classroom, you can cement and check for understanding by pairing loose parts with a comprehension prompt.

1. Place containers of loose parts in a student-accessible space.
2. Post/prompt with the comprehension check. For example,
   a) How did the United States' feelings about World War II (WWII) involvement change from 1939 to 1943?
   b) What does the human heart look like?
   c) What are the character's internal conflicts thus far?
   d) What are the duties of three government branches?
3. Once the prompt is shared, the students must gather loose parts and design/show their response. They may collaborate with partners or first work individually.

4. After a set moment of "play time," present the students with a manner in which to share their loose parts design. Options might include:

   a) Taking a photo, submitting it digitally, and writing an explanation/legend
   b) Pair-share discussions explaining designs
   c) Causal stand-and-deliver presentations in small groups, by volunteers, or to the whole class.

Samples of Play

In this sample of loose parts play, my sophomores had been studying *Fahrenheit 451* and were presented with a prompt checking for comprehension about the character, Mildred. Loose parts pictured include a paper plate, a colored paper, play-doh, a Lego figurine, and magazine cutouts. In order to show an understanding that Mildred is a TV-obsessed woman who is unaware of

Figure 5.2 Students use loose parts play to depict a content understanding of *Fahrenheit 451* by Ray Bradbury.

nature and the destruction of books, this student pair designed a huge screen and placed their Lego minifig facing it. The figure's back, conversely, blocks the green grass and looming fire (Figure 5.2).

Student-Facing Instructions

Project these instructions to incorporate this play-based approach in your secondary classroom:

> Let's play to build our knowledge! Today we will use "loose parts" (random, assorted items) to review our understanding of _____.
>
> Please use your choice of loose parts to build an answer this prompt:
>
> You may refer to your course notes/books as you design your answer. Be prepared to explain at least five specific choices you made. We'll design for ____ minutes.

Application across Secondary Disciplines

Business Education	Utilize small cups and popsicle sticks to make financial models or budgeting scenarios, helping students visualize financial data in a tangible way.
English Language Arts	Utilize magazine cutouts and string to connect key elements of plot, character, and theme.
Informational Technologies	Introduce basic programming concepts by having students use Lego pieces to create interactive models.
Math	Use small cups, popsicle sticks, and beads to create visual representations of mathematical concepts like fractions and proportions.
Multilingual Language Learning	Incorporate paper plates and magazine cutouts into storytelling activities. Ask students to share their narratives in the learned language.
Science	Have students use Lego pieces, paper plates, and more to build models of cell structures or chemical reactions.
Social Studies	Utilize magazine cutouts and string to create visual timelines of connected historical events.

References

Jones, J. P. & Southern Early Childhood Association. Using Concrete Manipulatives in Mathematical Instruction. *Dimensions of Early Childhood* 45(1), 18–23 (2017), https://files.eric.ed.gov/fulltext/EJ1150546.pdf.

Larbi, E. & Mavis, O. The Use of Manipulatives in Mathematics Education. *Journal of Education and Practice* 7(36), 53–61 (2016).

Stockman, Angela. "Make Writing Studios – Angela Stockman." 8 May 2014, https://angelastockman.com/writers-studios/.

6

Additional "Child's Play"

The AP US History learners have folders full of Civil Rights readings and Cornell note-taking guides covered in information. Their content-knowledge of this American era is new but they're confident; the topic is fresh yet familiar. And, instead of a more traditional lecture today, the students find picture books from the elementary school library spread across the front table as they enter the classroom. Learners partner up and each pair is handed a book: We Are The Change *by Harry Belafonte goes to the girls in the front right.* Choosing Brave *by Angela Joy is passed to the boys at the middle table.* Small Shoes, Great Strides *by Vaunda Micheaux Nelson goes to the left, and other books—like Levinson's* The Youngest Marcher *and Hook's* If You Were a Kid During the Civil Rights Movement—*make their way to awaiting partners in the back of the room.*

As intrigued students—some who haven't held a children's book in years—quietly page through the colorful pages, their teacher shares that today learners will cement their advanced knowledge of the Civil Rights moment with the inclusion of child-like play. They're high schoolers, though, so their learning goal for the day isn't to simply read the elementary-level stories. Instead, they'll enjoy the picture books with their partners–while also examining what content details are new, withheld, or understated. "Here's a guide for your thinking," the teacher says as he passes out a worksheet. The learners take the paper, find quiet spaces, and smile together as they read children's books in that innocent, pictures-out posture their kindergarten instructors once used.

DOI: 10.4324/9781003591924-7

Rationale

Recent Pew research suggests that of the average teenager's daily 5.5 hours of leisure time, just over three of those hours are spent staring at a screen (Livingston 2019). Social media posts circulating across older generations would have us believe that "gone are the days" of young people running around outside and, generally speaking, engaging in nonelectronic play.

While the mother-in-me might argue that the creative tinkering and spatial thinking of *Minecraft* does, in fact, offer value, playing solely or "alongside" (rather than "with") peers does negatively impact our learners. In the seemingly-gone leisure time—when older children created kick-the-can teams or coordinated a pickup game of baseball, such collaborative, playful interactions supported social and individual development. These experiences also helped prevent the mental health obstacles like anxiety, loneliness, and depression that pair with more isolated play today (Pollak et al. 2023). Using what, at first glance, might also be perceived as "toys of yore," secondary educators can reap the rewards of peer "playdates" while concurrently building needed content knowledge.

How to Play

In short, "children's play" is as simple as reframing a regular classroom activity to include a toylike element typically used by younger children. These "toys" need not be expensive or complex. Instead, most items can be found on a shelf in your local Dollar Store or laying around the home of any parent. Like "loose parts," these could be objects like chalk, play-doh, picture books, etc. Unlike the independent creation that "loose parts" play encourages, though, this approach is more structured and introduces the objects into the classroom with a sophisticated purpose. For example:

◆ Chalk/Dry Erase Markers
   These writing "toys" can be easy, low-pressure replacements for documents or worksheets—while providing community audiences, too. In the 7.1 photo, student writers had just studied impactful choices in diction and syntax and were moving into narrative essays. Transitioning from these lessons, they composed their own versions of the famous "six-word story" that supposedly Hemingway made legendary with: *For sale: baby shoes. Never worn.* Instead of submitting their

Figure 6.1 Secondary-level writers "publish" in chalk at their high school's front entrance.

finalized six-word compositions on paper or digitally, though, the learners grabbed some chalk, went outside, and playfully decorated our school's front sidewalks. At my school, mathematical equations, Spanish vocabulary, and more from colleagues' class content can be found as visitors stroll up to doors, too. Dry erase markers also often easily wipe off classroom tables and windows—despite the surfaces not being a "special" whiteboard kind. Instead of using paper, playful educators can invite learners to write directly onto desks and glass.

◆ Play-doh
Play-doh can allow abstract concepts to be represented tangibly. Like the loose parts play in the last section, play doh is an inexpensive and tangible way to have students demonstrate a specific understanding. For example, if reviewing Spanish vocabulary for activities, you might offer a word and then ask students to "show" it. You say, "jugar fútbol americano," and they model a football, etc.

Figure 6.2 Students use dry erase markers to record textual evidence directly onto their classroom table

◆ Picture Books

Like the anecdote at the chapter's start, children's book can present advanced content in unintimidating ways. English teachers might use picture books to introduce literary themes and styles, if written by the same author. Before my seniors study the sophisticated novel *Sula* by Toni Morrison, for example, I ask them to analyze an assortment of Morrison children's books. They observe thematic commentary, author-style, (illustrator intent), and cultural considerations—just as in a novel study—but with the quick, tangible texts. Additionally, students can review thesis statements by composing about the children's books; these same claims, quite beautifully, can also be applied directly to Morrison's novel. With *Peeny, Butter Fudge*, for instance, one past group of students noted that the nontraditional family structure of matriarchal leaders and household mess was, despite first glance, supportive of its children—building a parallel understanding about Hannah and Eva Peace's seemingly chaotic home.

Additionally, children's books can also introduce abstract concepts through active participation. My first-year teaching *Rosencrantz and Guildenstern Are Dead*, I struggled to articulate the "Theatre of the Absurd" term before our reading of the play. I knew I wanted to introduce students to this type of drama before our studies, but I could only offer the traits of such pieces; I struggled to make the topic tangible. The next year, I grabbed random picture books off my own children's book shelves, dumped the texts on a workstation at school, and prompted the class: take a book and make the characters self-aware. Suddenly, writing or acting out the dialogue of characters knowingly trapped in the pages of books made absurdity less abstract. Since then, my teammates and I have used the *Henry* picture books by D. B. Johnson to make transcendentalism more concrete for struggling students. We've used picture-book allegories (especially those by Dr. Seuss and Eve Bunting like *Riding the Tiger*, *Terrible Things*, *Sneetches*, *Yertle the Turtle*, etc.) to introduce that complex literary form and so forth.

Samples of Play

Figure 6.3 Pumpkins replace paper in these "Lit-o-Lantern" examples of child's play.

Besides the examples noted above, I've tried various silly and seasonal "toys" like the fall pumpkin pictured here. In this activity, the students first annotated a unique passage from Yaa Gyasi's novel *Homegoing* that introduces a character. Then, the students captured their understanding of the characterization on pumpkins instead of paper (with permanent markers). Later, we shared our "Lit-o-Lanterns" with one another to extend the whole class's knowledge (Figure 6.3).

Student-Facing Instructions

Since these instructions will differ depending on the child's play "toy," here are student-facing slides for the pumpkin annotations. As always, consider projecting these instructions to incorporate this play-based approach in your secondary classroom:

Let's "play" with prose points on pumpkins!

1. Annotate your pass with stylistic noticings on:
   - Motif(s)
   - Tone of verbs
   - Parallelism and anaphora
   - Loaded connotation
   - Webs and/or echoes to other chapters
   - Other stylistic observations
2. Next, annotate your pumpkin with ideas on the author's stylistic depiction of this character. Record:
   - Perceived motivations of this character
   - Internal versus external conflicts
   - Stylistic choices

Application across Secondary Disciplines

Business Education	Use chalk to draw out customer journey maps or marketing funnel diagrams. Add play-doh-made brand logos to incorporate real-world examples.
English Language Arts	Read a children's book to practice gathering textual evidence. Then, have students make visual representations of the created themes using play doh.

Informational Technologies	Utilize play doh to model algorithms or coding concepts. Or, read a children's book and transcribe a character's movements into code.
Math	Use colored chalk to diagram geometric proofs or solve equations on outdoor surfaces. On a rainy day, turn windows into worksheets with dry erase markers.
Multilingual Language Learning	Use picture books in the target language to introduce cultural themes and vocabulary.
Science	Use play-doh to model biological processes such as cell division or chemical reactions. Or, read a picture book that describes scientific phenomena and then rewrite the elementary-level language with advanced content vocabulary.
Social Studies	Have students read children's books about historical events. Then, apply advanced content understanding by extending or challenging accuracy in the narration and pictures.

References

Livingston, G. "The way U.S. teens spend their time is changing, but differences between boys and girls persist." *Pew Research Center*, 20 February 2019. https://www.pewresearch.org/short-reads/2019/02/20/the-way-u-s-teens-spend-their-time-is-changing-but-differences-between-boys-and-girls-persist/.

Pollak, I., et al. A Systematic Review of Intervention Programs Promoting Peer Relationships Among Children and Adolescents: Methods and Targets Used in Effective Programs. *Adolescent Res Rev* 8, 297–321 (2023). https://doi.org/10.1007/s40894-022-00195-4.

7

Float Ideas

Caleb has always struggled with self-advocating in his learning. He gets nervous asking questions of his teacher and often thinks he understands the course content, but then later—on unit assessments at the end of studies—will find he had oversimplified the key ideas. Today, though, his freshman English Language Arts teacher is trying a playful knowledge-check about the first three chapters in John Steinbeck's Of Mice and Men—*and Caleb's confidence will soar after he learns what proper "folds" his mind still needs to make to best comprehend the characters of George and Lenny.*

Simple copy paper sits on a desk as the ninth graders enter their ELA classroom. Written on the whiteboard are seven comprehension-check questions about the opening pages of the novel they received last week. As a bell-ringer, the teacher prompts the students to share designs of the most effective paper airplanes they've ever learned. Caleb, a self-proclaimed math-science brain who sometimes dazes in this literature class, enthusiastically shows his table-mates the infamous Nakamura Lock construction. "Now," his teacher transitions, "we're going to use these designs to check our comprehension of John Steinbeck's book so far. Look at my list of questions and select one to answer. Let's use paper airplanes to ensure smooth flying through the novel." Caleb grabs his pen and a piece of copy-paper eagerly.

DOI: 10.4324/9781003591924-8

Figure 7.1 High school seniors float their ideas about a literary text.

Rationale

The World Health Organization has suggested that some 80% of teens do not meet the recommended plateau for playful, physical activity each day (Herting et al. 2017). We also know, through the expertise of individuals like Antronette Yancey of UCLA's Center to Eliminate Health Disparities, that learners "pay better attention to their subjects when they're active" physically (Neighmond 2006). Here's an easy, no-prep approach to move students—and papers—around your classroom.

How to Play

1. Gather blank computer paper for each learner in the class.
2. On a student-facing slide, pose questions—either one at a time or as a list from which students choose:
   - For content-building, these questions could prompt comprehension of the subject studied. For instance, what branches create the American governmental system or what is the function of the respiratory system?
   - (To later use this play-based approach as skills application, these questions could prompt analytical thinking. For instance: how would you evaluate Plato's definition of justice or to what extent is the ending of *Fahrenheit 451* hopeful?)

3. Provide each student with a piece of paper. Ask them to place their name at the top of the page and then answer one or more questions on the page.

4. After writing time, have the students fold their papers into paper airplanes. (If desired, you could play a quick tutorial video to guide their folding.)

5. Have the students "float" their insights across the room.

6. Prompt students to move about the room, pick up a classmate's airplane, and unfold the paper after returning to their desk.

   - If content-building, the students could affirm or correct their classmates' answers. They can then answer another question on the paper and repeat the float-correct-write process as many times as desired.

   - If extending as a skills application, the students could extend or counter their classmates' answers. They, too, can then answer other questions as desired by restarting the float-correct-write process.

Samples of Play

As an English Language Arts teacher, my students' content-building often centers around knowing the characters and plot of a text—a needed first step before we're able to conduct literary analysis around the effects of those authorial choices. I pair comprehension-check questions with airplane flights—allowing the students to each assess the answer of the person before them. At the end of our playtime, we return the papers to their original designers.

Student-Facing Instructions

Project these instructions to incorporate this play-based approach in your secondary classroom:

Let's playfully "float" our ideas!

Directions: Answer the question(s) below with specific terms and explanations from our current unit.

When prompted by your teacher, fold the ultimate paper airplane and float it across the room.

Then, unfold, read, and respond to your classmates' ideas.

Application across Secondary Disciplines

Business Education	Prompt with questions about the defining traits of economic systems.
English Language Arts	Prompt with plot comprehension questions.
Informational Technologies	Prompt with basic coding functions and the related language.
Math	Prompt with a multistep problem.
Multilingual Language Learning	Prompt with translating short sentences.
Science	Prompt with categorizing specific organisms within biological system classifications.
Social Studies	Prompt with causes/impacts of historical events.

References

Herting, Megan M., & Chu, X. Exercise, Cognition, and the Adolescent Brain. *Birth Defects Research* 109(20), 1672–1679 (2017). https://doi.org/10.1002/bdr2.1178.

Neighmond, P. "Exercise Helps Students in the Classroom." *NPR*, 31 August 2006, Exercise Helps Students in the Classroom. https://www.npr.org/2006/08/31/5742152/exercise-helps-students-in-the-classroom.

8

Research Role-Playing

The Calculus seniors seem to grow exponentially more disengaged as each month moves closer to graduation. They began the year studying limits and continuity, derivatives and functions. Today, though, they walk into their classroom and are surprised that construction paper, string, tape, and markers have replaced the usual grid-paper pile.

"This content did not simply appear in your textbooks," their teacher begins. "These mathematical ideas are instead the human-made creations of theorists like Gottfried Wilhelm Leibniz and Sir Isaac Newton," she continues. "In order to better consider the development of content we study next, today I'd like you all to 'meet' Newton and ask him about his discoveries during the Plague, a time also known as the Year of Wonders."

Confused, the seniors giggle over the potential of a posthumous conversation, some sitting up more straightly from their literal (and metaphorical) slumps. Following the teacher's guidance, the students first quietly read background information about Newton and his studies on their laptops. Then, voices and excitement grow without bound as some learners begin fashioning an apple with red paper and prism-like glasses of tape and string.

DOI: 10.4324/9781003591924-9

Rationale

After Friedrich Froebel categorized play as object manipulation, crafting occupations, and song expression, the progressive kindergarten movement of the 1900s further emphasized the importance of dramatic play as a learning avenue for children. Early education classrooms of today contain pretend-play locations like miniature kitchens and general stores. Dramatic role-playing has also maintained a presence within social-emotional learning—with adolescents and adults alike playing roles while studying crisis management, conflict resolution, restorative communication, and more. Employing role-play in content-building can "connect subject matter with visceral memory… supporting all learning dimensions of cognitive, affective, and behavioral development" (Aura et al. 2023). In classrooms that first build felt safety, students who role-play as the content they're learning can more actively store and retrieve key ideas.

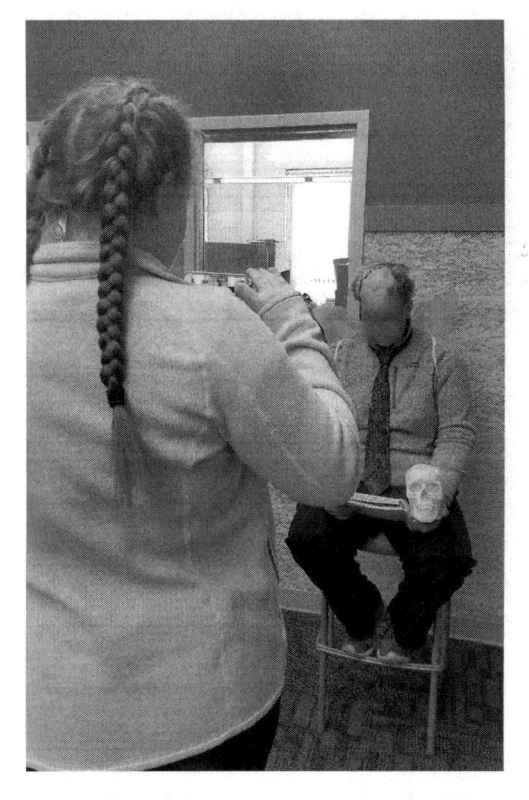

Figure 8.1 Students use assorted props and costume pieces to role-play as an author they've researched.

How to Play

First, please note that it would never be appropriate to role-play as a marginalized person/group nor as someone whose actions/words harmed other people. This approach should not be considered if researching about enslaved people, studying fascist regimes, etc. If unsure if your topic is appropriate to role-play, it is not. Some topics should never be made playful.

If topic-appropriate, first focus your students' content-building on some human-connected subject that can be researched. For instance, if studying a historical event, you could connect to the experiences/ideas a person living through that event might encounter. If studying a book, you could connect to the author's life and times. If studying a scientific discovery, you could connect to the individual who originated the thought. Then, prompt your students' content-building and role-playing in phases:

◆ Phase one: Research. Use a guiding question like "what ideas and experiences would a young person living in Boston but born in England encounter in 1775 as they determined their opinions about the American Revolutionary War? Set parameters on the sources that you'd like your students to use to answer this prompting question. Ask students to record their findings in a low-stakes manner, such as on a piece of notebook paper or in a printed organizer.

◆ Phase two: Collaboration. Place the students in small groups and prompt them to share their research with one another. If any disparities in content facts appear, the students should triangulate with an additional source.

◆ Phase three: Role-play prep. Give the students access to construction paper, tape, string, and markers. (An alternative approach could be to share a costume/prop box with students from which they could to use items.) For their preparation, ask the students to "become" the person they've researched in a symbolic way. That is, they should not mimic the person's appearance. Instead, they should build the individual's persona through choices that reflect their research findings. For instance, a person of 1775 might have a split heart between their birth country of England and their new hopes for America. To represent this conflict, students could draw a split heart on construction paper—one side showing the British flag and the other side depicting the colony's flag. They might then cut and tape the heart onto a classmate.
  – In the past, I've had students "become" their researched topics as entire groups—with each group member representing some symbolic insight.

- – In the past, I've also had groups select a willing volunteer to fully "become" the researched persona individually.
- ◆ Phase four: Role-playing. Finally, ask the students to role-play as their research topic. You could have each group introduce and explain their symbolic persona. Additionally or alternatively, you could also have prepared questions for your symbolic persona—returning to the initial research prompt. For instance, if researching ideas and experiences of 1775, your follow-up questions for the role-play might be:
  - – Do you think the American colonies will likely gain independence? Why or why not?
  - – What message might you offer King George of England?
  - – Which writers and thinkers of your time do you most admire?

Based on their research, students should prepare and then respond to these follow-up questions as best as they're able. They could present live or video-record their responses as a group.

Samples of Play

Figure 8.2 Students role-play their understanding of Plato's *Allegory of the Cave*.

The Figure 8.1 picture demonstrates authorial research my ELA students role-played before beginning a literature circle study. My teammates and I prompted the researched role-play and then asked the symbolic personas what personal events inspired their writing, what historical events inspired their writing, and what about humanity did they most fear. (The literature circle novels were all dystopian.) In another course and as depicted in Figure 8.2, my students needed content-knowledge about Plato's *Allegory of the Cave*. In lieu of asking them to read a description of this concept, I first had them research and then—with ceiling lights out and lamplights on—do a role-played performance of the allegory while explaining their findings.

Student-Facing Instructions

Project these instructions to incorporate this play-based approach in your secondary classroom:

Let's role-play to better understand our studies!

Phase One: Research
Directions: Using the resources provided or the online resources of your choice, spend ten (10) minutes finding as much information as you can to answer this question:

  Record your research findings on a page in your notebook. You do not need to use full sentences but should bookmark your resources.

Phase Two: Collaboration
Directions: Meet with your group-mates. Spend ten (10) minutes sharing the information you each found to answer this question:

  If any information found by one student conflicts with information found by another, please look for a third resource to clarify which is correct (or why there might be a disparity).

Phase Three: Preparation
Directions: With your group-mates, use your research to "become" _____.

  You should not try to physically look like the person. Instead, you should symbolically represent the person.

  For example, if your person values education, you could design a graduation cap for them to represent a passion for schooling.

  ◆ Use the construction paper/props to design/attach at least five symbols that show your researched person. Be creative!

◆ You may have one group member volunteer to become the person individually, or you may each represent some element of the person.

Phase Four: Role-Playing
Directions: As instructed and with your group, "become" your person. Answer the following questions based on your research:

Application across Secondary Disciplines

Business Education	Research and role-play as an expert marketing professional from a specific company based on the brand's identity.
English Language Arts	Research and role-play as your studied author.
Informational Technologies	Research and role-play as a famous information technology (IT) icon.
Math	Research and role-play as a mathematical theorist who discovered a key formula.
Multilingual Language Learning	Research and role-play as a cultural icon.
Science	Research and role-play as a scientist who wrote a famous theory.
Social Studies	Research and role-play as a common person from a specific historical time/event.

Reference

Aura, I., Järvelä, S., Hassan, L., & Hamari, J. Role-Play Experience's Effect on Students' 21st Century Skills Propensity. *J Educ Res* 116(3), 159–170 (2023). https://doi.org/10.1080/00220671.2023.2227596.

9

Scavenger Hunts

Earlier this week, the Spanish 1 students recorded vocabulary and practiced pronunciation of commonly used adjectives. They reviewed translations of basic colors and then added descriptive words like "alto/a" (tall), "pesado/a" (heavy), "viejo/a" (old), and "estrecho/a" (narrow). Señor Flores knows that his learners will store this language best if engaged in an activity that challenges their linguistic use at just the right level, so he prompts retrieval playfully this Friday morning. One willing student—in each group of four—opens a digital scavenger application on their phone and finds photo challenges listed. There are even some harder one descriptions using two or more "adjectivos" for additional points.

Enthusiastically, the Spanish 1 class spreads out across the school on the hunt for objects they can connect to their vocabulary. One team takes a photo of a chalkboard that appears "mas viejo" than the teenagers themselves—while a second group walks past determined to capture the Tiger statue at the school's entrance that is "naranja." At the conclusion of the photo hunt, Senor Flores stores the best pictures to use during later review and offers "dulce" to the winning team—one that earned impressive points with a picture of a gym locker that was simultaneously "estrecho y pesado y de color café."

DOI: 10.4324/9781003591924-10

Rationale

Finnish game scholar Markus Montola claims that scavenger hunts first originated in ancient folk culture—perhaps as a cousin to the more dramatic treasure hunt experience (Marx 2012). In America, scavenger hunts became especially popular in the 1930s after the release of the film *My Man Godfrey* and in the 1980s outrageous scavenging boomed on college campuses. In 2011, the online platform Goosechase was conceptualized at a Canadian hackathon, and scavenger photo hunts moved into the digital sphere (About Goosechase 2024). The science behind scavenger hunts' appeal focuses largely on the collaboration and problem-solving parts of the play. When the hunt's challenge falls within Vygotsky's Zone of Proximal Development and includes intentional student-to-student collaboration, the players' engagement is heightened and content is mastered (Vygotsky 1978).

How to Play

1. Determine a means to connect your course content to physical locations within your space (classroom, wing, school, etc.). You could physically print and post vocabulary words that would not otherwise be around the building like cell parts of mitochondria, cytoplasm, and ribosomes. If doing so, be sure to add a bonus item alongside the vocabulary words (symbol to capture, word to make a secret phrase, etc.). In some cases, like multilingual learner words or the advertisements/posters that my students have searched for while learning persuasive strategies, the physical presence of your terminology might already be just hanging around.
2. Create a paper guide (physical) or mission bank (digital via Goosechase) of content-connected definitions.
   - If you'd like your students to physically write down the definitions, be sure to leave space for their writing. Include a spot for the "bonus" items, too—to ensure they're hunting and not simply looking up definitions.
   - If you'd like your students to use Goosechase for photo submissions, head to goosechase.com/how-it-works for simple setup instructions.

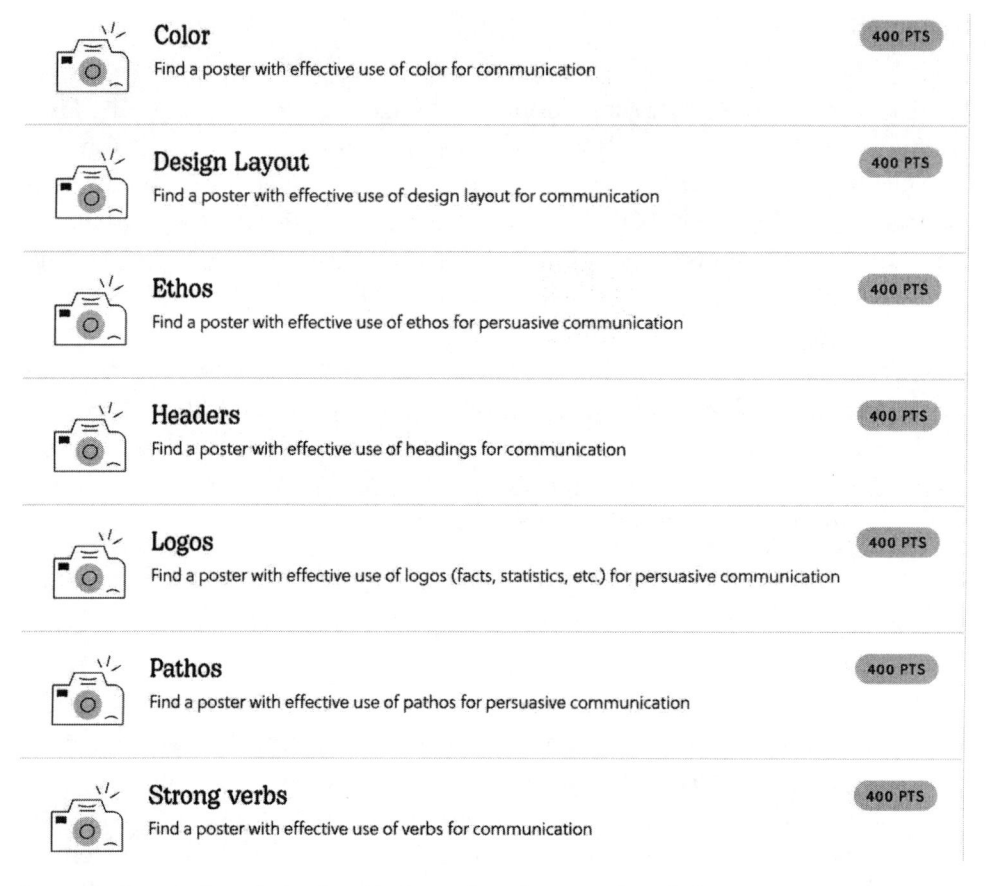

Figure 9.1 Design elements are listed in Goosechase for students to find during a poster-focused scavenger hunt in their school.

3. Assign teams, set behavioral expectations, and send them off hunting!
4. After the scavenger hunt, use the students' experiences and/or photo submissions in reteaching and retrieval!

Samples of Play

In my English Language Arts classroom, I've used scavenger hunts to find persuasive writing strategies with sophomores, present renaissance vocabulary with college-credit seniors, and more. In addition to content-building play, I've also used this playful approach to celebrate and reflect on an entire course at the end of the year. Currently, my International Baccalaureate (IB) English seniors play a scavenger hunt right after their college-credit exams. Prompts include missions like (Figures 9.2–9.4):

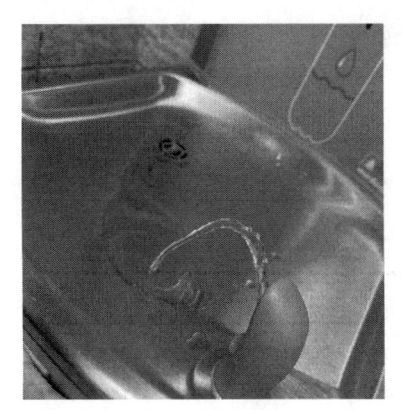

Figure 9.2 Mission *Everything I Never Told You* Memory: Take a picture with an item Celeste Ng made symbolic. Consider, but do not limit to, eggs, physics book, cookbook, water, etc.

Figure 9.3 Mission the Man Behind the Scenes: All things IB happen, thanks to the efforts of Mr. M. Write the man a quick "thank-you" note for his hard work running this program. Leave the note on his door or desk.

Figure 9.4 Mission *Metamorphosis* Memory: Franz Kafka writes that Gregor woke up as a bug. Take a picture of one—created or found.

Student-Facing Instructions

Project these instructions to incorporate this play-based approach in your secondary classroom:

Let's "scavenger" through our materials!

Today, we will review _____ by conducting a scavenger hunt around the school. A successful scavenger hunt looks like:

- ◆ Finding the listed items successfully
- ◆ Staying with our teammates
- ◆ Collaborating to locate clues
- ◆ Respecting the people and learning happening around us
  - Walking
  - Using quiet voices
  - Not interrupting classes
  - Staying focused on the scavenger hunt itself.

You have ___ minutes to locate and capture clues hidden around ___. At 0:00 please report back to this classroom and be ready to share your findings. Best of luck!

Application across Secondary Disciplines

Business Education	Search for marketing strategies across school posters.
English Language Arts	Search for persuasive strategies across club signs.
Informational Technologies	Search for—and then label as code—basic instructions posted throughout the school.
Math	Post answers and then prompt students to search for them with matching equations.
Multilingual Language Learning	Search for vocabulary items (parts of building, school terms, action words, colors, etc.).
Science	Post answers and then prompt students to search for them with matching scientific terminology.
Social Studies	Post answers and then prompt students to search for them with matching historical facts.

References

"About Goosechase." *Goosechase*, 2024, https://www.goosechase.com/about.

Marx, P. "The Hunter Games." *The New Yorker*, 25 June 2012, https://www.newyorker.com/magazine/2012/07/02/the-hunter-games.

Vygotsky, L. S. *Mind in Society: The Development of Higher Psychological Processes*. Harvard University Press, Cambridge, MA, 1978.

10

Matching Card Games

While they know the words will pop up often in adulthood, these high school students still struggle to engage enthusiastically with their Personal Finance vocabulary. "IRA" feels like a decades-later term and "asset" and "investment" blur in many learners' minds. While their Business teacher knows that flashcards and definition lists can assist her learners in storing these real-word concepts, today she sets up the classroom with plastic spoons and homemade cards.

After a quick review of the rules of Spoons, she stands back and sips her coffee as learners excitedly pass squares of paper and yell over utensil-grabbing motions. Like making financially savvy decisions with money, the students decide when to "hold" and when to "fold" their vocabulary-filled cards—all while learning important definitions as they play.

Rationale

Card games have been at "play" around the world for centuries. Chinese literature of the 10th century describes dominos/cards. Italian merchants of the 1300s received such games from Islamic traders. And even King Charles VI of 14th-century France is rumored to have commissioned an artist for the creation of a special deck of cards (Parlett 2024).

While many card games can be played within a classroom while building content, a particular favorite of my learners has been *Spoons*, a 1990s variation of the older *Donkey* game. In this version, students match terms with

DOI: 10.4324/9781003591924-11

definitions in order to learn course content—but in a competitive, playful approach that's sure to add energy and laughter to your classroom.

How to Play

Game's objective: To match two pairs and successfully grab a spoon. (Also, to avoid being the last player to attempt to grab a spoon, only to instead find them all take by other players.)
Players: Three or more learners
Materials needed:

- ◆ A deck of content cards—usually 13 different topics (with two term cards and two definition cards for each topic to total 52 cards)
- ◆ Spoons (one fewer than the number of players)

Setup:

1. Arrange the spoons in the center of the table so everyone can easily reach them.
2. Shuffle the deck and deal four cards to each player.
3. Place the rest of the deck face down to form a draw pile.

Gameplay:

1. The dealer takes the top card from the draw pile, looks at it, and either keeps it or passes it to the next player on their left.
   - If the dealer keeps the card, they must discard one card from their hand, passing it face down to the next player.
   - If the dealer passes the card, they draw a new card from the deck to keep their hand at four cards total.
2. Each player, in turn, either keeps the card they receive (discarding another card) or passes it along, keeping their hand at four cards.
3. Play continues around the table, with each player passing one card at a time until someone collects four of a kind (two terms and two matching definitions).
4. As soon as a player has four of a kind, they sneakily and silently grab a spoon from the center of the table.
5. Once a spoon has been taken, all other players must quickly try to grab a spoon. (Sometimes play can continue for a while longer, as players intensely watch their cards and forget the spoons.)

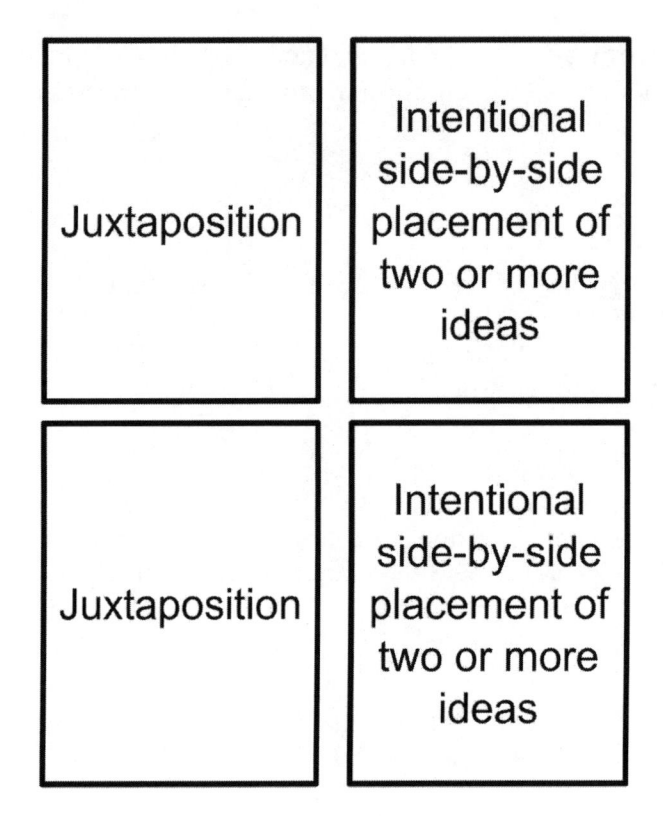

Figure 10.1 Two pairs of literary device cards to make four of a kind.

Rules:

- Players must only hold four cards at any time.
- Players cannot touch the spoons until someone has collected four of a kind and grabs one first.
- Cards are passed one at a time and face down to the player on the left.
- The game can move quickly, so players should pay close attention to when someone grabs a spoon so as to grab one too and not be "out" of the round.

Samples of Play

My students use this game to study the literary terms and stylistic devices we need to apply in advanced Literature courses. On a back bookshelf of my classroom, I have a few gallon baggies with the gameplay instructions, a deck of literary term cards, and plastic spoons. Sometimes we play during class time as directed by me. Sometimes the students grab a bag and study as a small group during work time or study hall.

Student-Facing Instructions

Project these instructions to incorporate this play-based approach in your secondary classroom:

Let's play a card game to build our content knowledge!

Your objective: To match four cards (two terms and two definitions) and then successfully grab a spoon.

- ◆ You may only hold four cards at any time.
- ◆ You cannot touch the spoons until someone has collected four of a kind.
- ◆ Cards are passed one at a time and face down to the player on the left.
- ◆ When someone grabs a spoon, you can grab one too and not be "out" of the round.

Application across Secondary Disciplines

Business Education	Match key terms and their definitions.
English Language Arts	Match literary devices and their effects.
Informational Technologies	Match coding language and its functions.
Math	Match mental-math formulas and their answers.
Multilingual Language Learning	Match words and their translations.
Science	Match vocabulary and its meanings.
Social Studies	Match historical facts/dates/figures and their descriptions

Reference

Parlett, D. "Playing Cards | Names, Games, & History." *Britannica*, 27 April 2024, https://www.britannica.com/topic/playing-card.

11

Escape Rooms (Digital or Physical)

Rae enters her Social Studies class excitedly each day–History has always been a favorite area of study—but today the class starts in an especially intriguing way. Instead of greeting his learners at the door like usual, Mr. Xiong sits at his desk seemingly consumed by some electronic teacher-task. When the bell rings and he still hasn't begun with his regular "Today in History" fact, Rae's eyes navigate to the projector's screen to find, quite literally, a clue. Instead of the expected date-related historical event, she reads—aloud to herself—this riddle:

> *I once divided, but now I unite,*
> *where East and West had stood in fight.*
> *Find me in this classroom light,*
> *and today's escape room will take flight!*

"What's an escape room?" the boy next to her murmurs. An answer comes from another student across the room. "East and West divided?" Rae ponders to herself. "As in, the wall that separated Western democracies and Eastern communism in the Cold War?"

"The Berlin Wall," she speaks aloud, and the classroom's eyes move to a model of concrete watchtowers, colorful graffiti, and barbed-wire strands that sits atop Mr. Xiong's bookshelf. Leaning against this physical symbol of division protrudes a tan envelope marked with a red "Spies Only" stamp. The students look at their teacher, who now can't hide that he's watching them with a large grin, and three learners jump up at once to open the second message.

DOI: 10.4324/9781003591924-12

Rationale

In truth, our current research about escape-room play's effects on students' knowledge retention is sparse. The first actual escape room appeared in Japan in 2007, and the playful experience didn't make its way into classrooms until even more recently (A Brief History Of Escape Rooms 2022). A meta-analysis by Belova and Lathwesen from the University of Bremen, Germany, does find, though, that student participation in escape-room play increases positivity, self-efficacy, and self-reported feelings of "joy," "satisfaction," and "fun" in learners (Lathwesen and Belova 2021). Their findings also suggest that escape rooms blend especially well into STEM courses studying subjects Chemistry, Mathematics, Physics, and Biology—as these fields highly value experiential thinking. (Anecdotally, I think escape-room play has prompted fruitful and joyful learning in my English Language Arts classroom as well.) And any activity in which happiness and learning blend feels worthy of description in this play-based book.

How to Play

Figure 11.1 A locked box holds treats for students who can find its code in a variety of escape-room-inspired clues.

When first incorporating escape-room play into your secondary classroom, I'd suggest using or tweaking pre-built games found on a platform like Breakout EDU (www.breakoutedu.com/). Some material on the website does cost money, but there are also free games and trial opportunities. After seeing variations of escape-room play, you'll learn what puzzles you'd like to include in your own physical or digital games. (Or you just might luck out and find online a pre-built game to use, like one of the many curated here by the Madison County Library: www.madisonlibrary.org/at-home/digital-escape-rooms.)

After you've found/designed a series of puzzles—with each pointing to the next clue—you can pair these escape-room elements with your unit content. You could thematically connect your puzzles to the topic you'd like your students to understand, like in the physical sample below in which the learners do a word search for items to bring to an interview. Or, more simply, you could add a fact to each puzzle and ask students to collect these content facts as they go. For instance, the word search might be for random words, but at the bottom there's an explanation of interview clothing recommendations that the students read and/or copy onto a guide.

At the end of the puzzling, successful escape-room players usually unlock some sort of prize to enjoy. As most secondary schools have lockers, you could connect with your main office to inquire if an empty locker might be used to store a treat. You'd then list the locker number and combination on your last clue. The Breakout EDU website store also sells complete Breakout kits with resettable locks like the one in my picture. Teachers sometimes use filing cabinet drawers or simple totes with locks, too.

Samples of Play

In truth, creating an escape room—be it digitally or physically—takes more preparation work than any of the other playful approaches found in this guide. A simple Google Site with an embedded Form can be used to create a digital escape room, though. And once you've built the page, you can simply return to it year after year.

For example, a digital escape room that I created to pair with Section I and Chapter 5 of William Golding's *Lord of the Flies* can be found here: https://sites.google.com/view/lotf-challenge-4-break-away/home?authuser=1, if you'd like to give it a play. *Spoilers: For the "word lock," I used a rebus from a puzzle-making website to represent "parachutist" (under the "Beast from the Air" link). For the three-digit number lock, I hid numbers in the Symbolic Considerations pictures. For the four-digit number lock, I transposed the morse code found right above "Test Your Understanding," and the directional lock is the pattern of up/down/ left/right language in the Hints for Analysis section.* Repeat these puzzles yourself as desired.

With a few extra supplies and some printing/posting, physical "escape rooms" can also review content and engage high school learners in play. Below is a full game—with setup instructions, gameplay, and materials—that teaches students the non-spoken elements of a strong professional interview. Topics covered include when to arrive before the interview, what to wear, what to bring, who to offer as references, and how to follow up after the meeting. I've used this physical escape room with juniors—usually on two half-class teams—and usually follow up the game with a comprehension check about the content.

"INTERVIEW DAY" ESCAPE ROOM

Created by Amy Heusterberg-Richards

Level: High School
Topic: Interview "Extras" (attire, time arrival, nonverbals, etc.)
Timing: ~90-minute block class (groups break out in around 60 minutes)

Materials needed:

- Faux dictionary lockbox (could be changed to other container)
  (Recommendation: Amazon's Stalwart Book Key-Portable New English Dictionary Hidden Mini Safe for Traveling)
- Puzzle box (could be changed to another container)
- Red lens *(Recommendation: Amazon's 9 Pack Gel Filter Colored Correction Gel Light Filter Transparent Color Film Plastic Sheets, 11.7 by 8.3 Inches (Red))*
- Invisible ink pen flashlight *(Recommendation: Amazon's 4 Pack Invisible Ink Pens with UV Light)*
- Some electronic means (iPads, computers, etc.) for students to research interview topics as prompted
- Large paper and markers
- Folder and envelope
- Prize (in locked box with combination, if desired)

Materials included (See the end of instructions):

- Interview outfit options (Copy as is or download color version from routledge. com/9781032970486)
- Clocks (Copy as is or download color version from routledge. com/9781032970486)
- Crossword puzzle (Copy as is or download color version from routledge. com/9781032970486)
- Red lens message paper (Copy as is or download color version from routledge. com/9781032970486)
- Reference check form (Google Form link: https://forms.gle/sfuffTCGM7vCpAfe6)

Setup:

1. Print the interview outfit papers, the clocks, and the crossword puzzle.
2. Place interview outfits and "select the five…" message inside a folder.

3. Inside the locked dictionary, place the flashlight and the "always double-check your interview time" printed message.
4. Outside the locked area of the dictionary, but inside the cover flap: place the "Your interview today is at 9:00…" paper message.
5. Write a clue location message on the 8:45 clock in invisible ink. (For example, I usually write "look outside the classroom door" and then place the next clue there.)
6. Hang all the clocks around the room.
7. Place the key to the (already locked) dictionary in the puzzle box.
8. Place the "Thanks for arriving on time!" message in an envelope. Hold onto it until you give the message to students during the activity.
9. Post the crossword in the location you described in invisible ink. (For example, just outside the classroom door.)
10. Print and post the red lens message paper in color ink.
11. Place this message in the class' digital location, and add the link to the reference check form: *Congratulations! You've dressed for success, showed up on time, brought the perfect materials, and wow-ed our interview committee with your nonverbal presence. We'd like to move you forward to our last round of consideration. Could you please offer three people to serve as references? These should be people who can positively speak about your character, work ethic, and job-related skills.*
12. Leave out large paper and markers for the thank-you note.

Escape room experience:

1) Teacher places opening message on whiteboard/projector:
   Today in class, your team will have to research/make such choices as you puzzle through this Interview Day Escape Room challenge. Each correct decision will move you closer to the information you need to unlock the job (see also prize box). Collaborate well and move as a team. Like most special occasions, your first step for today is to select the best outfits.
2) Teacher hands the group a folder with the photos of potential interview outfits.
3) Students place five correct outfits together and spell: DI-CT-IO-NA-RY.
4) Students locate the dictionary lockbox. It is locked, but inside the cover flap is the message letting them know their interview begins at 9:00 am. Students research to learn that the general recommendation is to arrive 15 minutes early to an interview.
5) Students take down the 8:45 clock. They read the passcode message to their teacher.
6) When students tell the teacher "Hello. I'm [insert name], your interview candidate," teacher gives an envelope with the message to open a puzzle box located near teacher phone.

7) Students figure out how to open the puzzle box and find the key to the dictionary.

8) When students open the dictionary's inside box, they find the invisible ink flashlight and message to double-check their time.

9) Students shine the flashlight on the 8:45 clock to receive the next location message. (For example, invisible ink says to look just outside the classroom door.)

10) At the next location--for example, posted outside the classroom door—students find a crossword with what to bring with them to an interview.

11) Students complete the crossword. Then, they ultimately notice that the remaining letters spell: *Research interview nonverbals. Then, sit down in chairs and show them.*

12) Students research nonverbal interview skills. Then, they sit with such bodies until the teacher is satisfied. When students show effective nonverbals, they receive a red lens.

13) Students notice the red lens-needed message posted somewhere in the classroom. They use the red lens over the paper and are told to go to the class' digital location (Schoology, Google Classroom, Canvas, etc.).

14) The digital location message reads:
Congratulations! You've dressed for success, showed up on time, brought the perfect materials, and wow-ed our interview committee with your nonverbal presence. We'd like to move you forward to our last round of consideration. Could you please offer three people to serve as references (link)? These should be people who can positively speak about your character, work ethic, and job-related skills.

15) Students go to the Google Form reference link.

16) On the Google Form, students select "High school teacher," "Coworker," and "Coach/advisor."

17) Once those three references are typed in, students can submit the form. They receive the message: Thank you so much for these references. You seem like a truly wonderful candidate. We'll be contacting you soon with our final decision. (Until then, use the large paper provided to write a "follow-up" email offering appreciation for the interview experience. Use mentors from online as needed. Submit your "email" to your teacher as soon as possible. As long as it contains all the needed components, you will receive your next—and last!—clue.)

18) Students go to the large piece of paper and write a thank-you "email." They then submit the paper to the teacher when done.

19) When the teacher is content with the thank-you note, they give students a prize and/or winning combination.

Materials to Copy:

Select the five outfits you deem most
appropriate for a professional interview.

Then, puzzle on.

DI

CT

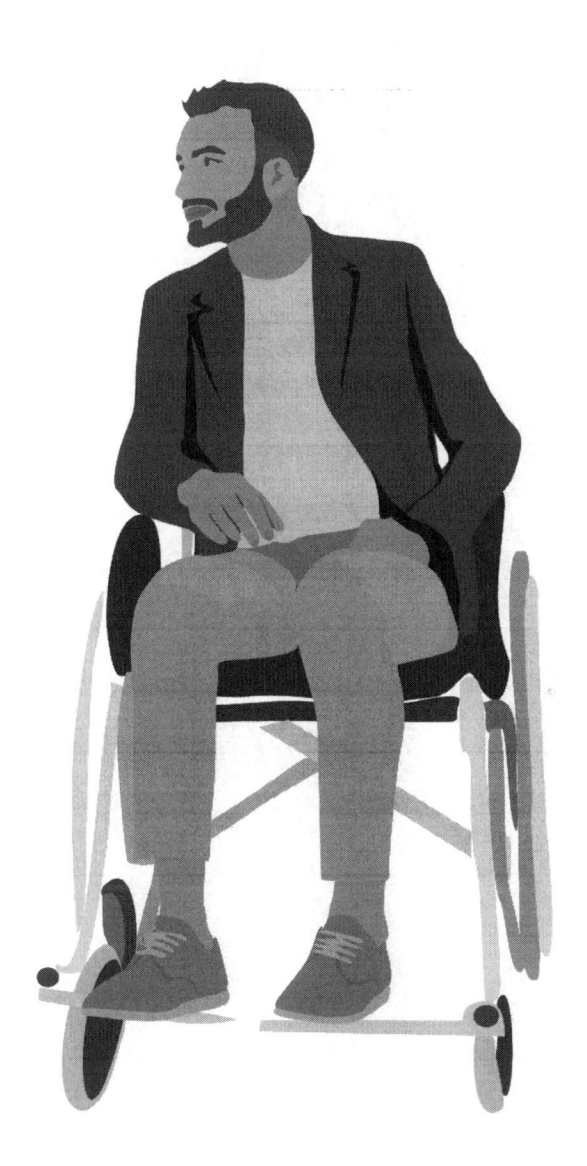

10

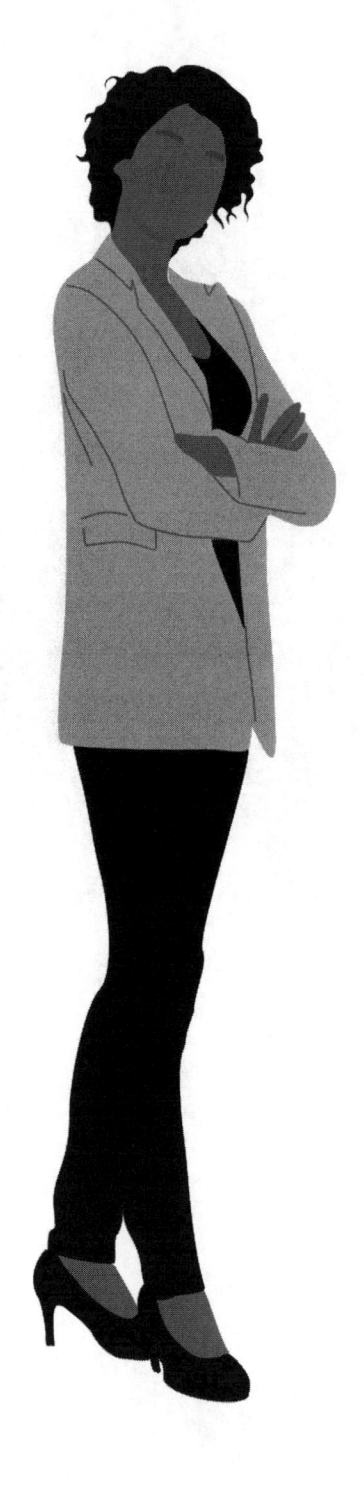

NA

RY

ST

ER

AP

BE

OU

Your interview today is at 9:00 am. You are familiar with the location and do not have to travel far.

At what time should you arrive at the building in which the interview takes place?

Select the correct clock and read its passcode to your teacher.

- *If nothing happens, you've selected the wrong time. Try again.*
- *If you're correct, your teacher will give you the next clue.*

Passcode: "Good morning. I'm here for my interview."

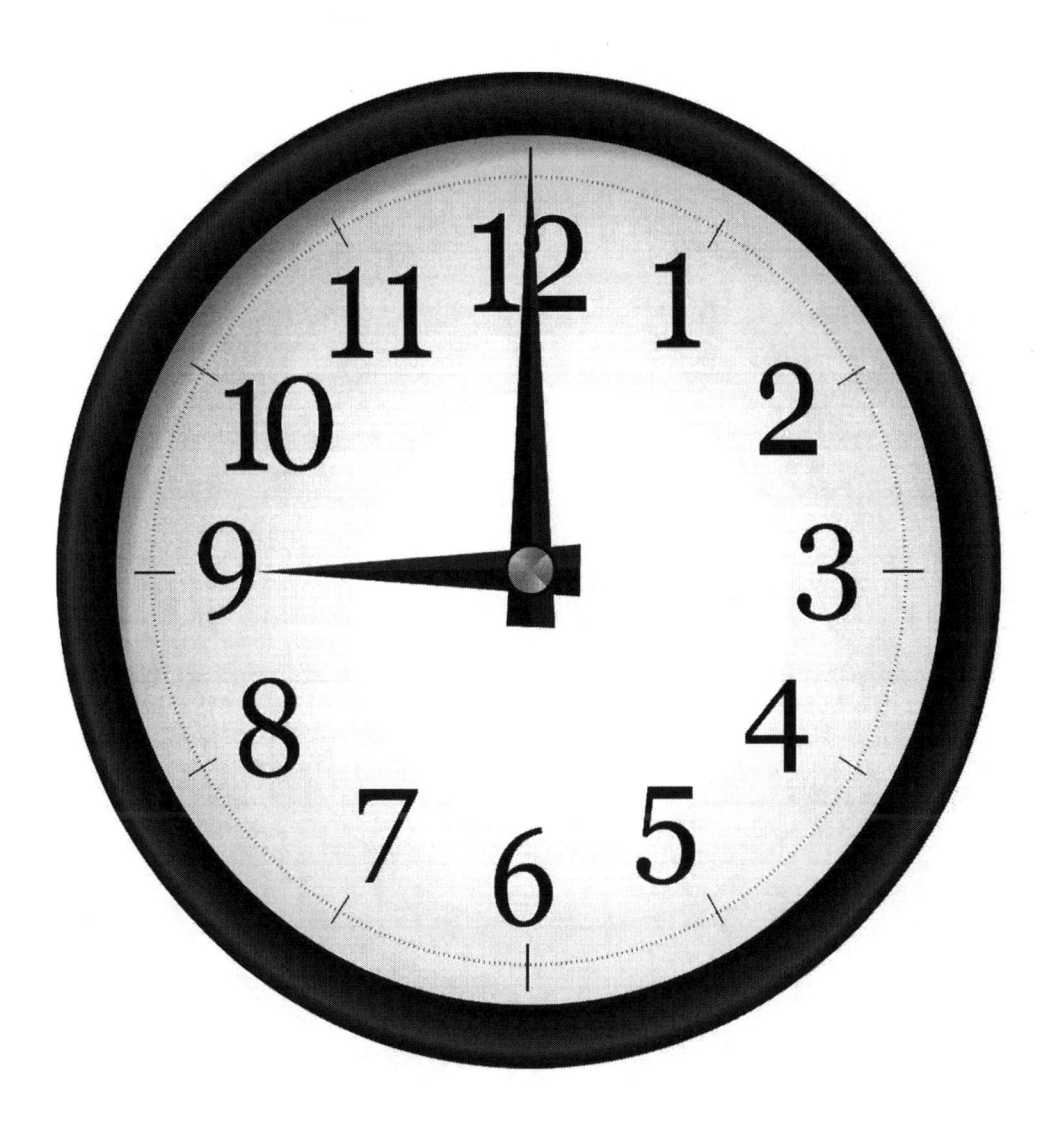

Passcode: "Hello. I'm [insert name], your interview candidate."

Passcode: "Hi! I'm here to interview with you today."

Passcode: "It's very nice to meet you. I'm [insert name]."

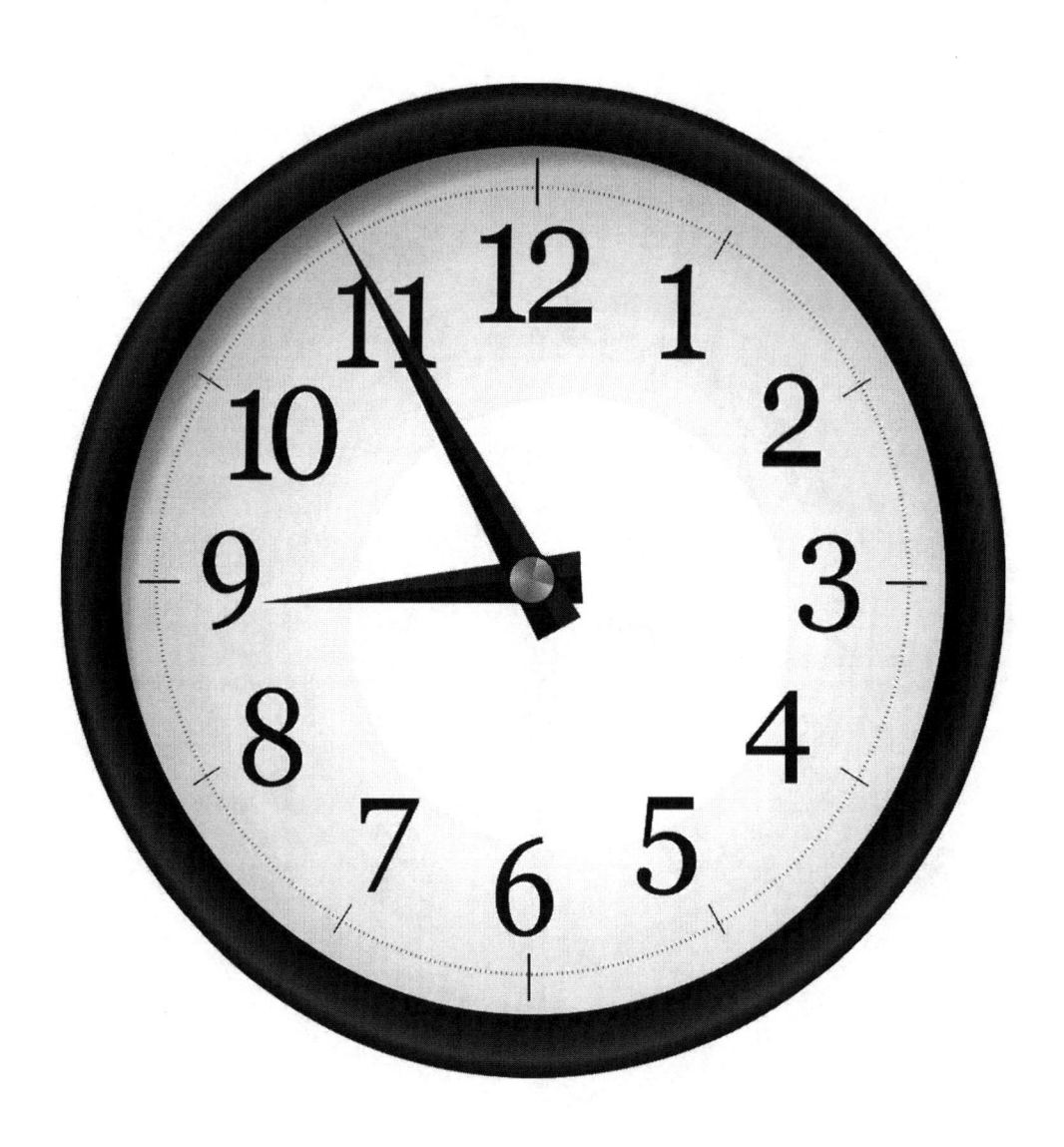

Passcode: "Hi there! I'm excited to interview with your company this morning."

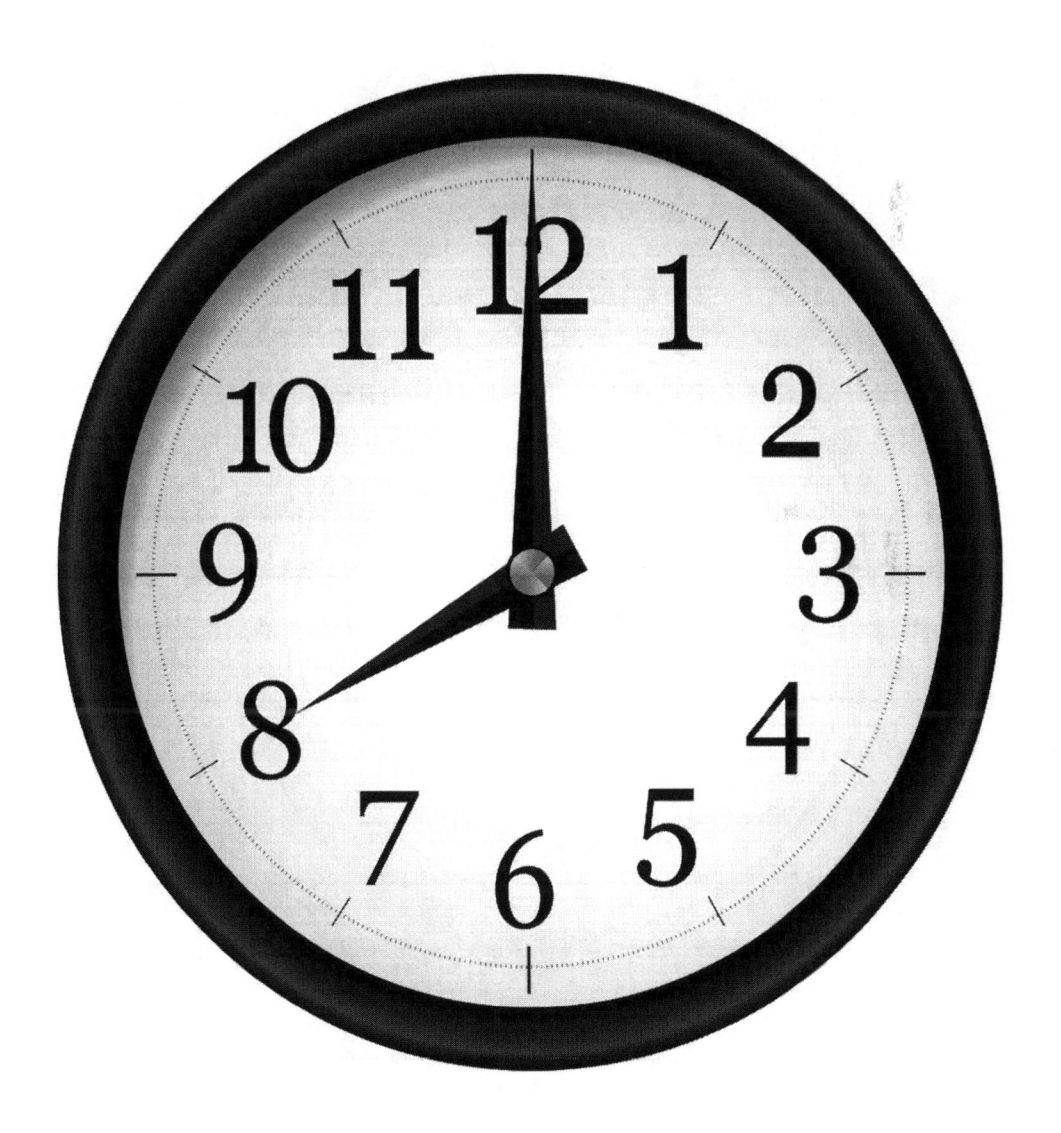

[Place the following inside an envelope]

Thanks for arriving on time! You're off to a great start!

Sometimes interviews begin with a skills assessment. These often connect to the job a person is applying for.

- A retail position might begin with a scenario quiz on how to best handle customers.
- An administrative assistant position might have a writing speed test or a phone call role-play.
- A tradesperson might be asked to build/repair a demo.
- As teachers, many of us had to take a personality test about how we build student relationships and/or teach a lesson in front of a panel.

In this "skills assessment," your task is more simple: Locate a puzzle box near the classroom phone... and open it.

Random tip: Always double-check your interview time the night before to ensure you remember the right time.

Materials to bring with you to an interview:

Business card *(if applicable)*

Confidence

Notebook

Pen

Portfolio *(if applicable)*

Questions

References

Resume

Water bottle

After you find the secret message,

start here to do

what you are told.

Word search grid:

E	W	L	O	R	H	C	E	L	O	B	H
C	O	N	F	I	D	E	N	C	E	U	S
T	E	Q	U	E	S	T	I	O	N	S	D
N	I	A	D	I	T	R	I	A	D	I	N
I	V	B	T	P	W	A	V	B	T	N	A
W	A	T	E	R	B	O	T	T	L	E	S
H	R	N	I	A	O	E	R	R	I	S	R
C	N	R	S	H	H	S	E	E	S	S	I
P	O	R	T	F	O	L	I	O	N	C	A
R	T	E	N	C	S	E	T	V	E	A	H
A	E	V	E	N	D	E	M	N	H	R	C
E	B	N	H	I	N	R	N	U	T	D	N
S	O	O	T	N	A	M	I	O	S	N	I
E	O	S	E	C	N	E	R	E	F	E	R
R	K	N	S	W	S	E	H	N	S	W	R

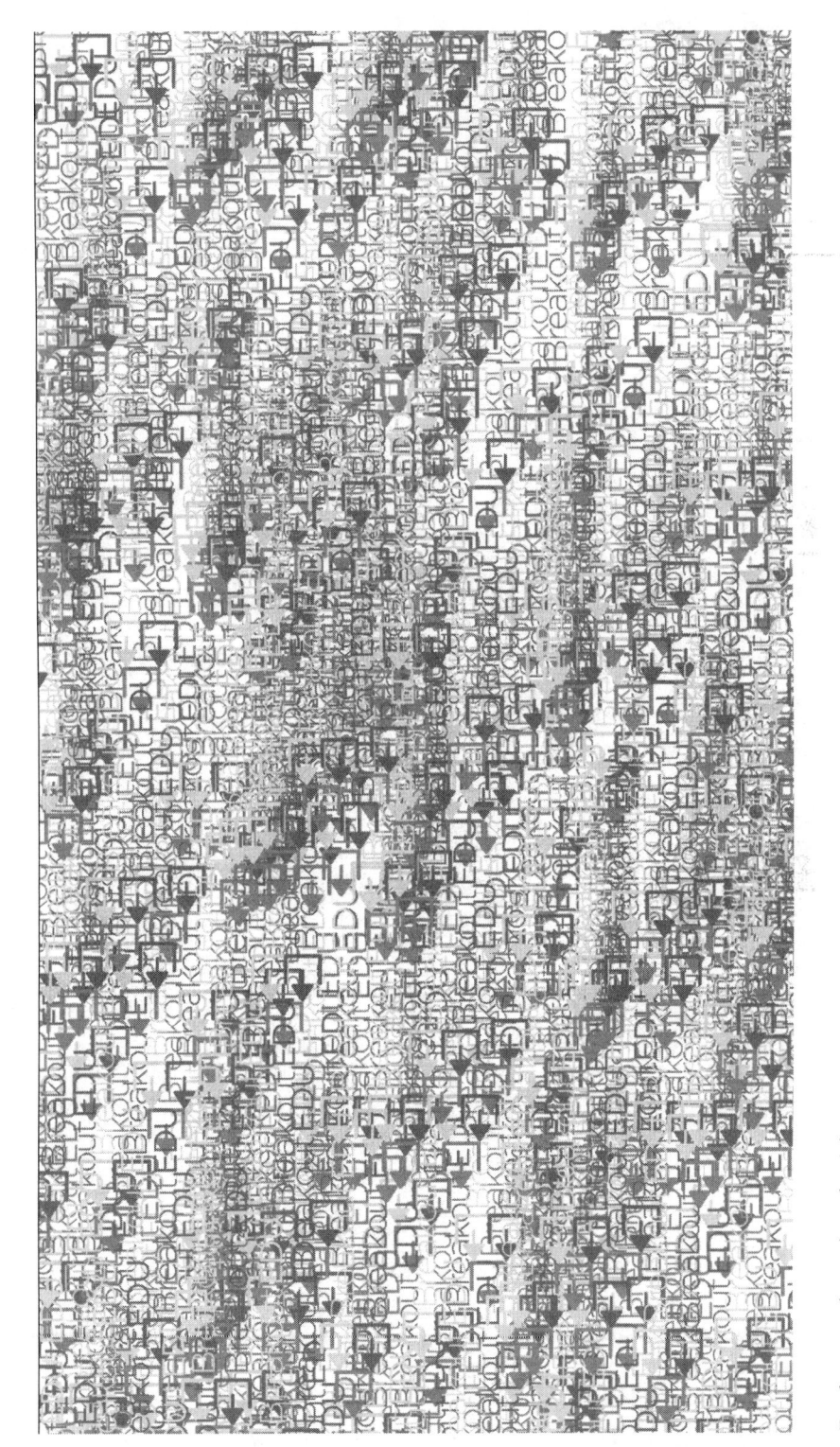

Background reprinted with permission from BreakoutEDU.

Student-Facing Instructions

Project these instructions to incorporate this play-based approach in your secondary classroom:

Let's play in an "Escape Room!" Today in class, your team will have to research and make informed choices as you puzzle through this _____ breakout challenge.

- ◆ Put your heads together and puzzle your way to an "escape." You have _____ minutes. The clues are all around you.
- ◆ Each correct puzzle answer will lead you to the next puzzle—and ultimately closer to the information you need to unlock the box prize.
- ◆ Collaborate well, read all material, and move as a team. Good luck!

Application across Secondary Disciplines

Business Education	Digital escape room about marketing plans: www.greatideasforteachingmarketing.com/marketing-plan-escape-room/
English Language Arts	Digital escape room about Shakespeare: docs.google.com/forms/d/e/1FAIpQLSfw8FgvQWkmRvuSs87xkj4xzipPe5bso81NA0Gt9krhsA5dHQ/viewform
Informational Technologies	Matrix-inspired digital escape room: docs.google.com/forms/d/e/1FAIpQLSfvlSynqTvt79MTKTu_Cw69pbly0BFP96qH9nEmpuP8lBqdQ/viewform
Science	Digital escape room about states of matter: sites.google.com/view/statesofmatter3-5/home
Social Studies	Digital escape room about the Titanic: docs.google.com/forms/d/e/1FAIpQLSeeRb0WYWFT5vy8Le00QptVKEeuBvBU76Td6K5h-h6ouHKlfw/viewform

References

"A Brief History of Escape Rooms." *Exit The Room, the Real Escape Game,* 21 March 2022, https://www.exittheroom.com/blog/a-brief-history-of-escape-rooms.

Lathwesen, C., & Belova, N. Escape Rooms in STEM Teaching and Learning—Prospective Field or Declining Trend? A Literature Review. *Educ Sci* 11(6), 308 (2021). https://doi.org/10.3390/educsci11060308.

12

Whole Unit Gamification

Though Asher and Eli are good friends, today they walk into their Biology classroom joshing one another about who's scoring better than whom. Their discussion doesn't surround their course grades as might be expected, though. Instead, their playful banter leads them to a paper scoreboard posted on the wall underneath a laminated "Cell Cycle Stages" diagram. Their quick glances reveal that, since last class, Asher's team has taken the lead in this unit's game—with his group now ranking two points above Eli's. The first boy grins and the second sighs, warning that the next "challenge" will be his team's to claim.

That next challenge on the scoreboard will, in fact, be tallied at the conclusion of today's class, their teacher announces. Asher and Eli smile at one another across the room as their respective teams begin "Challenge 3: Cracking the Genetic Code," with each group striving to correctly solve the highest number of Punnett Squares. Asher's team gets stuck on a question about a flower species, in which red petals (R) incompletely dominate over white petals (r) and result in pink petals (Rr) in the heterozygous state. They just can't determine the probability of offspring colors if two pink flowers were crossed. Eli's team, however, excitedly finishes all but two squares at the end of the set "play-time." The two friends walk up together to turn in their team submissions. They shake hands before navigating back to their desks for more structured learning the rest of the class period.

DOI: 10.4324/9781003591924-13

Rationale

Because there are many unique variables to measure, research on gamification and learning outcomes is officially inconclusive. As Sailer and Homner instruct in their 2020 meta-analysis, "gamified learning approaches focus on augmenting or altering an existing learning process to create a revised version… that users experience as game-like. Thus, gamification is not a product… [but] a design process of adding game elements" (Sailer and Homner 2020). Generally, though, this same study notes a positive, medium-sized correlation between gamified learning and successful student performance—especially with a focus on motivation. As such, endless resources exist online and in print about how to "gamify" classroom experiences. Some guides will prompt you to consider game lore, make student aviators, use gaming platforms, create complex quests, reward with leveled badges, and more. While those setups amaze me and likely motivate learners, the specific play-approach description in this book aims for low prep with still intrinsically and joyfully found results.

Figure 12.1 The flag of a winning team hangs near a scoreboard from a gamified unit.

How to Play

In short, my colleagues and I have simply and successfully used gamified play in high school courses by:

◆ Creating the teams—ours complete with names, flags, and anthems
◆ Explaining scoring
◆ Modifying practice lessons to be group "challenges"

Here's a more developed explanation for each of those steps:

1. Creating the teams: In my average class of about 24-28 learners, I typically run about six teams of four to five students. I do not personally allow my students to completely pick their group mates; instead, I use a Google form to request "three classmates with whom they'd most successfully work" and then build the teams myself, trying to include at least one person each student requested. To make the teams feel special, my colleagues and I prompt the groups to name their squads, decorate mini plastic flags, and pick victory songs.

2. Explaining scoring: Once the teams are set, I reassure students that their team performances within the gamified unit do not affect their individual course grades. They may receive individual scores on individual components, but the actual game-play intends to engage their interests, encourage their collaboration, and assist their learning through low-stakes but important content practices. I tell the teams how many game challenges there will be—usually around five or six for the unit—and show them the scoring process and board: If six teams are playing, the top-ranked team of each challenge receives six points, the second-ranked group receives five points, etc. (Figure 12.2).

3. Modifying practice lessons to be group challenges: The "challenges" that teams face are typically revised in-class practice activities. For example, before gamifying, my students might have used the early chapters of *Lord of the Flies* to understand the island setting of the novel. Rewritten as a "challenge," the groups receive a set amount of time and the task of using their books to draw the most accurate map of the island setting. At the end of the allotted time, I then collect and "rank" the maps—adding points to our scoreboard accordingly.

PERIOD ____

Team Name	Challenge 1 Fire Building	Challenge 2 The Masks They Wear	Challenge 3 Found Poem	Challenge 4 Beatty Breakaway	Challenge 5 Scattergories	Challenge 6 Group Quiz
		+	+	+	+	+
		Total:	Total:	Total:	Total:	Grand Total:
		+	+	+	+	+
		Total:	Total:	Total:	Total:	Grand Total:
		+	+	+	+	+
		Total:	Total:	Total:	Total:	Grand Total:
		+	+	+	+	+
		Total:	Total:	Total:	Total:	Grand Total:
		+	+	+	+	+
		Total:	Total:	Total:	Total:	Grand Total:
		+	+	+	+	+
		Total:	Total:	Total:	Total:	Grand Total:

Figure 12.2 A gamified unit scoreboard.

Samples of Play

Figure 12.3 To kick off a gamified unit in an especially playful way, students make a red-cup "fire" by stacking and collaborating.

Currently, my course teammates and I use a gamified unit to playfully engage sophomore learners in a study of *Fahrenheit 451* by Ray Bradbury. Like the steps noted in the How to Play section, we've revised in-class activities to function as scored, team "challenges." In the most playful (and admittedly least literary) challenge at the very start of the game, teams are given a set number of red, plastic cups and prompted to "make a fire" like our main character Montag's occupation. The goal of the challenge is to have the tallest "fire" structure at the end of five minutes (and points are ranked most to least for tallest-to-shortest builds). Ultimately, teams have to weigh whether they want to keep their structures at safe-but-sure heights… or push them to be the tallest, despite precarious balance risks. Such play consistently brings laughter and energy.

The gamified challenges that follow involve creating artistic representations of characters, capturing stylistic noticings of a passage, completing a digital escape room (as discussed in the previous section), taking a comprehension quiz, and—as student skills develop at the end of the unit—demonstrating symbolic analysis through a category challenge (as discussed later in "Play as Skills Application").

Student-Facing Instructions

Project these instructions to incorporate this play-based approach in your secondary classroom:

> **Let's make this unit a "game" to play!**
>
> Throughout our studies, you and teammates will be given learning "challenges." These challenges will be scored six points to one point each.
>
> At the end of the unit/game, the team with the most total points wins!
>
> (Please note: How well your team does in the game does not impact your overall course grade in any way.)

Application across Secondary Disciplines

Business Education	Organize team-based challenges of economic scenarios—with points for strategy, analysis, and presentation.
English Language Arts	Gamify poetry analysis by having teams identify and explain various poetic devices in selected poems—with points awarded for the most insightful interpretations.

Informational Technologies	Have teams compete in coding challenges, app creations, or program debugging—with points awarded for problem-solving and functionality.
Math	Create teams that compete to solve complex math problems—with points awarded for accuracy and/or speed.
Multilingual Language Learning	Gamify vocabulary and grammar lessons by having teams play games, create skits, or translate texts—with points for correct usage and fluency.
Science	With experiments or simulations, add points for correct hypotheses, detailed observations, and successful experiment outcomes.
Social Studies	Assign team challenges such as creating historical timelines, reenacting historical events, or debating historical perspectives—with points given for accuracy, creativity, and argumentation.

Reference

Sailer, M. & Homner, L. The Gamification of Learning: A Meta-Analysis. *Educ Psychol Rev* 32, 77–112 (2020). https://doi.org/10.1007/s10648-019-09498-w.

13

Playing with Content—Via AI Support

The AP Language students know how artificial intelligence can be used to write (against the school academic honesty policy) an objective summary or compose a rhetorical analysis. They don't expect their ELA teacher to encourage their use of an AI platform today in class, though. Timid looks are shared across the room as learners open their laptops and navigate to the website link posted on the board. Like drivers who pace below the speed limit yet find themselves pulled over, the students wonder if they might be in trouble for some unknown but still illegal act. Does their personal writing mimic compositions by AI? Does their grammar-checking extension actually cross the school's academic policy line? What is happening in the classroom today?

"You're not in trouble," the apparent mind-reading teacher quips with a soft voice. "We're using AI today to play a review game about the key rhetorical moves we've learned so far." He offers instructions and then the excited student-typing begins. "How do I get it to stop guessing 'paradox?'" one learner exclaims. "I'm describing oxymorons!" "Yeah. Well, try describing 'irony' without the word 'expected!'" another responds. Dreaming about an AP score report full of 5s, the teacher smiles and silently points to a poster with his simple classroom motto: "Master your words to master your world." The students chuckle and play on.

DOI: 10.4324/9781003591924-14

Rationale

Though analysis about artificial intelligence's (AI) impact on student learning is significantly young, what research does confirm is that AI allows for personalized experiences beyond what any single educator can achieve—especially within the time constraints of classroom hours. AI, when prepared with responsible surveillance and paired with ethical responsibilities, can provide "quantity and quality of communication… just-in-time [with] personalized support for large-scale settings" (Seo et al. 2021). In this approach, AI serves as an individualized play partner in a content-review game for high school learners (and as a digital coworker that tackles the game preparation for the teacher, too).

How to Play

> *** *Please note: I am composing this guide in the summer of 2024 and currently "playing" with ChatGPT 4. As technology quickly advances, the specificity of my ideas will also quickly become outdated. Regardless, this playful approach can be modified to best fit with the AI you, dear reader, have access while reading.*

Before play: Connect with your information technology (IT) department to discuss student access to AI platforms. Your students might have limited access on school devices and/or Wi-Fi and proactive steps can ensure your playful activity works when you want it to.

This guessing game engages AI as a partner for students who are studying specific vocabulary and/or content.

1. As a teacher, use the following prompt to ask AI to write you "off-limits" words connected to your content topic. Save and print the central word and off-limits words together on cards to share with learners.
   Hi AI, I'm a teacher who is helping high school students review content about [TOPIC]. I'd like the students to prompt you to guess specific words, but they'll be unable to use certain off-limits words. For example:
   - Topic: Literary Devices
   - Word: Anaphora
   - Off-limits words for students: Repetition, Phrase, Beginning, Speech, Rhetoric

 – Example Student Description: This is a stylistic device where the same word or group of words is used at the start of multiple lines or sentences to create emphasis and rhythm.
 I will share with you my list of words. Please provide five "off-limits" words for each. These should not make the description impossible but should challenge the students to think. Understand?

2. After AI works as a teacher's assistant building off-limits words, share the central word and these off-limits words on cards with students.
3. Then, ask the students to begin by prompting AI with the following:
 Hi AI, I'm a high school student and in class we're playing a game called AI Guess! Here's how it works:
 – *I will give you a description of a word related to our current topic of study.*
 – *There are certain off-limits words I cannot use in my description.*
 – *Your job is to guess the word based on my description.*
 Ready to play? Here's my description:

Samples of Play

I pretended to be a Social Studies teacher reviewing Civil War topics with my learners (Figure 13.1). I used the teacher prompt above and AI shared responses in return like (Figure 13.2):

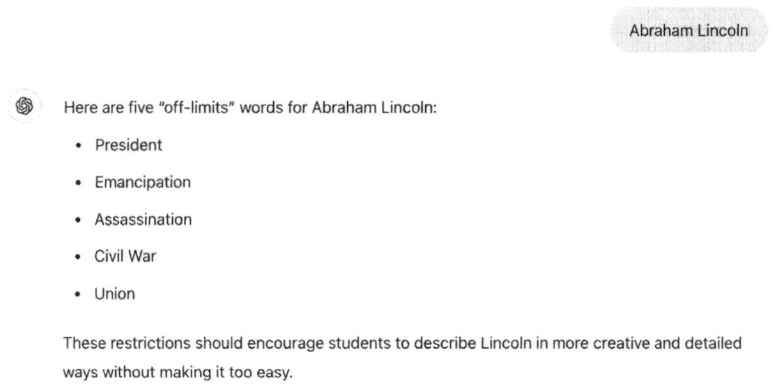

Abraham Lincoln

Here are five "off-limits" words for Abraham Lincoln:

 • President

 • Emancipation

 • Assassination

 • Civil War

 • Union

These restrictions should encourage students to describe Lincoln in more creative and detailed ways without making it too easy.

Figure 13.1 ChatGPT's OpenAI.

Compromise of 1850

Here are five "off-limits" words for the Compromise of 1850:

- Slavery
- Territories
- California
- Fugitive
- Agreement

This should prompt students to focus on the historical and political context of the compromise without directly referencing key elements.

Figure 13.2 ChatGPT's OpenAI.

Next, I assumed the role of a high schooler who was playfully reviewing this topic. I used the student prompt above and tried a description without the taboo words (Figure 13.3):

Hi AI, we're playing a game called AI Guess! Here's how it works:
I will give you a description of a word related to our current topic of study.
There are certain off-limits words I cannot use in my description.
Your job is to guess the word based on my description.
Ready to play? Here's my description:

I'm ready! What's your description?

This person was the leader of the United States when southern states and northern states fought over whether or not it was legal to enslave other people.

That sounds like Abraham Lincoln!

Yes! Let's plan again!

Great! I'm ready for the next round. What's your description?

Figure 13.3 ChatGPT's OpenAI.

Student-Facing Instructions

Project these instructions to incorporate this play-based approach in your secondary classroom:

> **Let's play with AI in a game called AI Guess!**
> - ◆ You will receive a word related to our current topic of study and five off-limits words you cannot use to describe this topic.
> - ◆ Without these words, you will use your content knowledge to describe your topic to AI. AI's job is to guess the word based on your description.
> - ◆ The student who is quickest at successfully moving through all their words and prompting correct AI guesses wins!

Application across Secondary Disciplines

Business Education	Economics teachers reviewing concepts like "supply and demand" could have students describe it without using terms like "market," "price," "goods," "services," and "balance."
English Language Arts	An ELA teacher might review the characters of a novel by giving students off-limits words that describe their direct characterization—prompting students to describe indirectly.
Informational Technologies	Computer science teachers building content on topics like "algorithm" might challenge students to describe it without using terms like "steps," "process," "instructions," "solve," and "problem."
Math	A math teacher could ask students studying concepts like "Pythagorean theorem" to describe it without using terms like "right triangle," "hypotenuse," "squares," "sum," and "legs."
Multilingual Language Learning	Language educators might generate off-limits words for vocabulary terms like *bonjour* in French without using words like "hello," "greeting," "day," "salutation," and "French."

Science	Science teachers studying "photosynthesis" could have students describe the process without using words like "sunlight," "chlorophyll," "carbon dioxide," "oxygen," and "glucose."
Social Studies	History instructors could use AI to create off-limits words about the "American Revolution" like "colonies," "independence," "Britain," "taxes," and "1776."

Reference

Seo, K., et al. The Impact of Artificial Intelligence on Learner–Instructor Interaction in Online Learning. *Int J Educ Technol High Educ* 18, 54 (2021). https://doi.org/10.1186/s41239-021-00292-9.

Section II

Play as Skills Application

Once students have solid understandings of content—the "what" of secondary subjects—learning can evolve into applying "how" to use this knowledge and exploring "why" it is important. Even in advanced studies, playful approaches can support the progression from foundational knowledge to practical implementation and critical examination. In fact, hands-on play and problem-solving scenarios actually help students retain educational concepts more effectively (Hand et al. 2021).

Traditionally, secondary educators have asked learners to apply skills through projects, essays, and presentations. While these opportunities to show developing competencies should continue to hold significant value in classrooms, adding playful chances to grow and apply skills can offer low-stakes, high-joy experiences for students, too. Research indicates that playful learning environments not only enhance student engagement but also deepen understanding and retention of academic content. As noted by Singer et al. in *Play = Learning*, "play is about how we learn, not just something we do when we stop working" (Singer et al. 2006). Integrating playful approaches into education encourages students to explore and apply their knowledge and skills in creative, meaningful ways.

Here are some low-prep, skills-application lessons to play in your secondary classroom.

DOI: 10.4324/9781003591924-15

References

Hand, B., Chen, Y. C. & Suh, J. K. Does a Knowledge Generation Approach to Learning Benefit Students? A Systematic Review of Research on the Science Writing Heuristic Approach. *Educ Psychol Rev* 33, 535–577 (2021). https://doi.org/10.1007/s10648-020-09550-0.

Singer, Dorothy G., et al., editors. *Play = Learning: How Play Motivates and Enhances Children's Cognitive and Social-Emotional Growth*. Oxford University Press, New York, 2006.

14

Pairing-Cards Game Variations

The end of a course is equal parts stressful and invigorating for teachers. Exhaustion comes from preparing summative assessments and finalizing course grades. Excitement, though, conversely stems from seeing how far learners have grown and how much knowledge they've gained. PE instructor, Casey Reed, feels both experiences as their freshmen walk into the Health classroom for the last week of the semester. As students pass, Mx. Reed hands each five slips of paper. "For a game about this course's materials," they offer when a questioning look is offered.

After the bell rings, students write Exercise Routines, Stress Management, Nutritional Guidelines, Hydration Strategies, and Sleep Hygiene as topics on their small papers—now turned into playing cards. Mx. Reed explains the rules and displays the first prompt on their screen: "You are a fitness coach designing a new program for teenagers who are looking to build muscle and improve focus. On what strategy would you first focus?"

Used to the noisy energy within the gymnasium walls, Casey quiets their urge to speak as they watch learners mentally sort units and units of studied Health curricula. Quietly, student after student lays a paper card on the group tables. Only when movement happens to flip over the card responses does Mx. Reed finally again hear the competitive banter well-known to PE educators. "Exercise Routines are the obvious choice for building muscle!" one student shouts. "But good nutrition will support muscle growth and mental performance! Remember salmon's omega-3s?" another learner refutes. The teacher listens on—tired yet fulfilled.

DOI: 10.4324/9781003591924-16

Rationale

In the five centuries since the standard 52-card deck made its debut, card games have dominated play across the world. Pairing-cards games—like the revolutionary *Apples-to-Apples* and boundary-pushing *Cards Against Humanity*—are a specific variation in which a prompting card is first drawn and then players lay potential best matches, aiming to create the funniest or most creative pairing. Typically during play, one person serves as the round's "judge" and selects their favorite match from the submissions. These pairing-cards games encourage creativity, humor, and strategic thinking as players consider how their cards will be perceived by the judge. The rounds are typically fast-paced, easy to learn, and highly social to play.

Additionally, research suggests that playing such card games strengthens cognitive functions like "memory, attention, perception, language, decision-making, reasoning, planning, judgment, knowledge, and visuospatial [thinking]" (Bhoos 2023). When Matt Kirby invented *Apples-to-Apples*, he actually was not intending to design a game. Instead, he meant to propel

Figure 14.1 Students pair tableaux poses with prompting cards in order to prepare for an advanced synthesis exam.

interesting conversations with his in-laws as they applied prior knowledge to discussion prompts like "who was the best author?" (Dekorte 2024). Ultimately in 1999, this complex and creative thinking earned the game a select prize from Mensa, the world's oldest and largest high-IQ organization (Mensa Mind Games 2024).

How to Play

Preparation Steps

To use pairing cards to develop your own learners' skills, you need to create prompts to show the whole class and pick a few applied content topics (four to six) to be interpreted by learners on individual cards.

1. Print enough small pieces of paper for each learner in your class to have a content topic card. For the sake of explaining, let's consider a Business teacher who has just taught students about basic marketing strategies. Each student might receive the same five content topic cards. These could include one for content marketing, social media marketing, search engine optimization, email marketing, and influencer marketing.
2. Next, write a few prompt "cards" (I usually use a projected slide) about which students will apply their content knowledge. For instance, the Business teacher would project the scenario:

   You are a marketing intern for a small but growing company that specializes in eco-friendly home products. The company is preparing to launch a new line of biodegradable cleaning supplies. These products are not only environmentally friendly but also effective and competitively priced.

   However, the company has a limited marketing budget and is relatively unknown in the broader market. What marketing strategy will best increase brand awareness and drive sales for the new product line?

Gameplay

After creating a few such prompts, your students are ready to play!

1. Place the students in groups of approximately five individuals. (Odd numbers work best.)

2. Give each student a set of content topic cards like that five marketing strategies in the example above.

3. Explain to the learners that they will be seeing prompts about which they will have to select/apply one of the content-topic cards. Ensure they know, though, that (like *Apples-to-Apples*) there is no single "correct" card. Instead, their play objective is to match what they *perceive* to be the best fit. When they decide on their desired content-topic card, the students should place these cards face down in the center of the table.

4. To ensure all learners can participate, there will not be a "judge" in this play variation. Instead, once every student has placed a content-topic card face down, they should flip over the cards and reveal what topic is in the majority. All the students who placed this majority-wins card would receive a point. For instance, in our Marketing scenario, if three students laid "social media marketing," one laid "content creation," and the fifth laid "influencer marketing," the three "social media" selectors would tally a point for this round.

5. Because the aim of this play is to apply skills, the best part happens next. At the end of the round, encourage students to explain their rationale for their selected cards to one another. For instance, the students who picked "social media marketing" might discuss the limited budget and social media's ability to target a specific audience—in this case, eco-conscious consumers. The student who selected the "content creation" card, though, might discuss the need for the company to establish itself as an authority in the eco-friendly product market. Additionally, the "influencer marketing" student might argue that the brand could quickly boost awareness by partnering with a similar-values influencer with a broad reach.

Samples of Play

In my own English Language Arts classroom, I have applied this prompting "card" and content-topic cards play in a variety of ways. With sophomores studying persuasive modes, I've offered a slide-projected prompt like "you'd like to persuade your teacher to give you an extension on a large project." Students, in turn, held and played three content-topic cards that said "ethos," "logos," and "pathos." In a literary analysis-focused class, my colleagues and I use famous book passages as prompts and give the students literary device topic cards. The passages all contain a variety of impressive authorial

Figure 14.2 Students hold "ethos," "logos," and "pathos" cards to pair with prompting scenarios that describe moments in which they would need to persuade others.

techniques, so the students first notice which literary devices are present and then apply that knowledge to infer which are most impactful to readers— their own selves and their playing group-mates. In Figure 14.1, my International Baccalaureate English seniors were preparing for an on-the-spot synthesis essay that helped determine college credit. I prompted with old essay prompts and groups of students used props and their own bodies to "lay" tableaux scenes from dramas we had studied. In this variation, the groups competed against one another, and I playfully joined the game as judge—selecting what I perceived to be the most creative and thoughtful frozen scenes for points (Figure 14.1).

Student-Facing Instructions

Since these instructions will differ depending on the prompts and topic, here are the student-facing slides for a literary passage sample. Project these instructions to incorporate this play-based approach in your secondary classroom:

Let's play a pairing-cards game!

Rules of the game:

1. A quotation will appear on this screen. Read through the quotation, and decide which literary device is most prominent to you. (The passages use more than one device.)
2. Place your selected literary device card face down on the table without speaking.
3. Your instructor will guide you as to when you and your group-mates should flip the cards over to reveal your answers.
4. Once all cards are flipped, take turns defending your selections and examining the impact of the literary devices within the quotation.
5. If you are in the majority picking a literary device, you earn a point. As a group, keep a running tally for each person's points.

Application across Secondary Disciplines

Business Education	Try the Marketing prompt and strategy content topics noted in the How to Play section.
English Language Arts	Try the passage prompt and literary device content-topics noted in the Samples… section.
Informational Technologies	Try to offer prompts about real-world tech problems and have students match them with relevant algorithms, programming paradigms, or development methodologies.
Math	Try prompting students to match mathematical problems to the most suitable solution strategies—such as algebraic manipulation, graphing, or factoring.
Multilingual Language Learning	Try offering conversation prompts that ask students to pair relevant vocabulary or grammatical structures.
Science	Try using prompts related to scientific scenarios and ask students to match them with appropriate scientific concepts or experimental methods—like choosing the best hypothesis to test in an experiment.

Social Studies	If teaching geography, try offering prompts about geographic phenomena and have students pair these with corresponding concepts or tools—such as types of landforms or mapping techniques.

References

"Bhoos | Sharper Brain: The Cognitive Benefits of Card Games." *Bhoos Games*, 17 March 2023, https://www.bhoos.com/blog/sharper-brain-the-cognitive-benefits-of-card-games/.

DeKorte, J. "Game Review: Apples to Apples." *People of Play*, 1 April 2024, https://www.peopleofplay.com/blog/game-review-apples-to-apples.

"Mensa Select Games." *Mensa Mind Games*, 2024, https://www.mensamind games.com/about/winning-games/.

15

Reasoning Tug-of-War

Upon entry to the classroom, the AP Euro students discover brown string and contentious claims scattered across pushed-together desks. They inquisitively take their seats and notice their names randomly sorted into "Team Tricolor" and "Team Crown" on the front screen. After morning announcements, Mr. Pasten hands out blue sticky notes to the Tricolor students and yellow stickies to those playing for the Crown. He declares the class will be "tugging" on historical strings to fight for the "right" side of the French Revolution. Instead of pulling with physical strength, though, the learners will use their intellectual might to apply knowledge from throughout this unit.

Team Tricolor students proudly hold their squares hued the first bold color of the flag. Team Crown learners majestically grip the gold seen in royal headpieces. When the play starts, both teams navigate the room's claims–with historical documents and handwritten notes in tow. Stopping by the table closest to the classroom door, two Tricolor students and two Crown opponents read a claim that weighs the future benefits and the current violence of the "Reign of Terror." Team Tricolor passionately scribbles evidence about the social equality to come. Team Crown tugs back with staggering statistics about guillotine victims. Throughout it all, Mr. Pasten quietly celebrates a historical tug-of-war that is seemingly as spirited as the revolution itself.

Rationale

The earliest play of tug-of-war—presumed from areas like Cambodia, India, China, Egypt, and Greece—consisted of hundreds of men pulling on ropes

DOI: 10.4324/9781003591924-17

to train as warriors and demonstrate strength. Especially favored in England and Scotland, a smaller-scaled, five-versus-five version of the game later reigned as an Olympic event for the first 20 years of the 20th century (Abt 2024). In this book's modified approach to the infamous game, students flex their cognitive muscles instead of their physical ones by offering complex reasons as "pulls" that support a central idea.

As key components of inquiry-based learning and general argumentation, reasoning-complexity skills help students analyze and evaluate evidence while considering multiple perspectives—in order to formulate claims and solve problems. Whether working with scientific, socio-focused, or literarily minded arguments, high school students need to be taught these reasoning methods that enhance their capability to develop well-supported justifications (Chowning et al. 2012). Such critical thinking ability will not only help learners best flex the skills related to course content; it can also tug us into a more well-reasoned, more just world.

Figure 15.1 Students use sticky notes to "tug" on opposing claims in this game of Reasoning Tug-of-War.

How to Play

For this playful skills application, you will need pre-prepared central claim(s) and studied content from which students can pull reasoning. The central claim may simply be one sentence shared by all learners or could be opposing interpretations of the same material. Ambitious teachers might place several claims/opposing pairs across a room for added reasoning-complexity and student flexibility.

1. The single claim could be written on a piece of paper. For instance, an English Language Arts teacher might claim "Hamlet's inaction stems from his intellectual depth and moral uncertainty." Two papers could also be used to present both affirmative and contrary claims opposing pairs. For example, a History teacher studying the USA's involvement in the Vietnam War might list "The United States' involvement in the Vietnam War was justified and necessary" and the opposing "The United States' involvement in the Vietnam War was unjustified and detrimental." (I'd recommend printing the opposing claims on two separate colors for student ease.)
2. To amplify the tug-of-war game experience, these central claims can quite literally be placed in the center of the "tugging" rope. I typically use a piece of yarn that reaches from one side of the table to the other. See the photo in Figure 15.1 as an example.
3. Before playtime, students should be placed on two teams—either by color (I hand out two colors of sticky notes) or by side (affirmative/ contrary). They should also have their content materials available for reasoning support (textbook, novel, notes, etc.)
4. During actual play, the students should navigate the room and offer "tugs" to support their side's claims. As demonstrated in Figure 15.1, my students write reasons on sticky notes and place them on the outside of the rope, "pulling" off their central claim(s).
5. After an allotted time, the team with the most complex-reasoning support "pulls" on their side of the rope wins the tug-of-war.
6. As desired, students can return to a few especially strong sticky notes and use these in more formal argumentation. For example, in Figure 15.2, my learners collect their two best sticky notes after our play, capture these on a worksheet, and then use these as evidence in analytical writing.

Name:_____ Period:_____
Literary Analysis
"Vandals" Analysis (in modified P-E-A form)

Point statement from "tug-of-war" activity: *(Rewrite it here.)*	Sticky note with evidence. *(Stick it here.)*

To continue practicing analytical writing, imagine you are finishing a P-E-A paragraph that supports this point statement about "Vandals." In the space below:

☐ Embed the textual evidence within your own writing (integrate with a lead-in)
☐ Cite the textual evidence using MLA format
☐ Write analysis that explains how the textual evidence supports the point's claim.

_____

_____

_____

_____

_____

Figure 15.2 Worksheet on which students gather sticky-note "tugs" and integrate them into continued studies.

Samples of Play

As an English Language Arts teacher, my students typically play tug-of-war with thesis statements and textual evidence from their literary readings. I've also had students write practice thesis statements themselves about a single story and then prompted to them play with a few of the strongest claims placed centrally over tugging "ropes." When learners are reviewing how to integrate textual evidence, they first just write quotations from the story as sticky-note "tugs. Then, I've followed up with a worksheet guide like Figure 15.2 to move students from skills-application play into skills-application formative assessment.

In my more advanced senior course, I've also offered claims that mimic college-credit exam prompts like "The authors describe the struggles of the human experience," "Art allows the authors to express their hope for humanity," and "The authors use descriptions of settings to impact interpretation of the texts." For these central claims, students must integrate textual evidence from multiple works as "tugs." After gameplay, the learners navigate the classroom—reading the collected evidence and reflecting how they might synthesize some sticky "pulls" together as a potential analytical essay.

Student-Facing Instructions

Since these instructions will differ depending on the topic, here are student-facing slides for a tug-of-war game using textual evidence from choice novels. Project these instructions to incorporate this play-based approach in your secondary classroom:

Let's play Textual Evidence Tug-of-War!

Objective: Leave the most (properly embedded) textual evidence to support your team's thesis statements.

Game rules:

- ◆ Use your choice texts for quotations.
- ◆ In the allotted time, move freely around the room.
- ◆ Leave the embedded textual evidence (lead-in + quotation) on your team-color sticky note. You must write a full sentence but do not need to further analyze/explain.
- ◆ The team with the most stickies on their side of the rope wins.

Application across Secondary Disciplines

Business Education	In a Personal Finance class, have students apply course content to "tug" at a claim like "Developing a personal budget is crucial for financial stability and goal achievement."
English Language Arts	After studying pieces of Romantic literature, have students apply course content to "tug" at a claim like "Symbolism enhances the depth and meaning of a text."
Informational Technologies	After reading about cybersecurity, have students apply course content to "tug" at a claim like "Implementing multifactor authentication enhances cybersecurity."

Math	While studying Calculus, have students apply course content to "tug" at a claim like "Understanding the fundamental theorem connects differential and integral Calculus."
Multilingual Language Learning	After studying a vocabulary set, have students apply course content to "tug" at a claim in another language.
Science	While studying Physics, have students apply course content to "tug" at a claim like "Newton's Third Law of Motion is fundamental to understanding interactions in physical systems."
Social Studies	After studying US Government, have students apply course content to "tug" at a claim like "Checks and balances maintain a fair and effective government."

References

Abt, Samuel. "Tug-of-War | Team Sport, Rope Pulling, Strength." *Britannica*, 2024, https://www.britannica.com/sports/tug-of-war.

Chowning, J. T., Griswold, J. C., Kovarik, D. N. & Collins, L. J. Fostering Critical Thinking, Reasoning, and Argumentation Skills through Bioethics Education. *PLoS One* 7(5), e36791 (2012). https://doi.org/10.1371/journal.pone.0036791.

16

Build-It Play

"As a culmination of our consumer behavior and product marketing unit," Ms. Billings announces to her crew of Intro to Business students, "we're going to build—and I mean that literally—a successful sale." To each table group, Billings passes out three, large trapezoid-shaped papers and one smaller triangle piece designed to cap a pyramid— or in this case, bottom-off the inverted Sales Funnel. "Let's show those skills playfully today. You'll 'brand' yourself a winner if the shapes you design are ultimately desired most by other groups. First, fill the largest trapezoid as 'Awareness.' Imagine how you'll make your consumers aware of a pretend product. Position the cutout wide-side up and record and/or draw your best ideas."

"Let's draw a Tik Tok symbol!" begins a girl with a Dutch braid as inverted as the funneled sales pyramid. "We can create awareness through influencer partnerships." "Yeah," adds a messy-haired boy, "And we can run broad-reaching ads on the platform, too." The group-mates collaborate excitedly and scribble intensely—until a play timer dings. They place their 'Awareness' papers on a side table for end-of-game review and grab the slightly smaller trapezoid. "Next round is building 'Interest,'" Ms. Billings directs, and the classroom erupts with productive voices—volumed at what a marketer might call "maximum exposure."

Rationale

Bloom's Taxonomy posits a thinking framework in which students move from remembering (level one) and understanding (level two) knowledge, like

DOI: 10.4324/9781003591924-18

the "Play for Content-Building" lessons prompt, to *applying* knowledge—and beyond! These later levels of Bloom's framework focus on advanced learning as the ability to analyze a topic by breaking it into smaller parts (level four) and then at the highest cognitive level (7), to restructure those same elements to create a new demonstration of thinking (UNC Learning Center 2024). Research also tells us that when students examine the smaller pieces of a topic, they feel less overwhelmed by the material and can extend their complex thinking more quickly (UMass Amherst 2024). Build-It Play skills application encourages restructuring and chunking of knowledge simultaneously.

How to Play

When "playing" with Build-It Play skills application, we ask students to deconstruct and then reconstruct their knowledge with specific "pieces." Different materials and shapes can allow students to "build" their reconstructed knowledge with varying focuses and levels of teacher prep work. What is consistent, though, is that this play offers joyful and tangible approaches to

Figure 16.1 Students build analysis about a novel with hexagonal cutoffs.

analyze and create knowledge. For example, my learners have constructed with playful shapes like:

- ◆ Hexagonal cutouts
  Moving beyond linear mind mapping, hexagonal thinking prompts students to synthesize more support, both in number of components and in complexity. For successful play with hexagonal cutouts, take a main topic and consider which parts it can be broken into. Label the hexagonal cutouts with these smaller pieces and then divide the hexagons across groups or an entire class. The students should first add corresponding knowledge to their individual hexagon(s). Then, they collaborate together to share knowledge and build a map—with touching pieces as ideas that can be directly linked. In my English Language Arts classroom, I have used hexagons to break apart and reconstruct an author's writing style and choices—like in Figure 16.1's pictured examination of motifs in a novel.
- ◆ Colorful notecards
  If your main topic has fewer but more detailed parts, consider using a colorful package of notecards to analyze and create. Then, play

Figure 16.2 Students build persuasive analysis using colorful notecards.

by giving students each color—one at a time—and prompting them to record as many details as feasible. After navigating all the topic parts, add an extra layer of competitive play into your classroom by asking students to literally build with the reconstructed pieces. For example, in Figure 16.2, my students were applying their knowledge of Aristotle's persuasive structure to practice an ACT essay prompt. The persuasive structure only contains four parts, so we assigned a notecard color—pink, orange, yellow, and green—to each. Students then captured their detailed knowledge about each part on the corresponding color and, at the end of the play, used all their notecards to attempt to build the tallest tower. (Our only agreed-upon rule: No extra materials like tape, glue, etc., could be added to the play.) At the end of the builds, the students with the tallest towers both shared their physical building strategies and their detailed understandings about the persuasive writing parts.

◆ Digital building supplies
Analytical discussion prompts can easily be changed into a playful building approach with the addition of a platform like Google Drawings. Students with editing ownership can manipulate objects on a copy of Google Drawings, so the teacher need to only make a master document and then share the link. In the Figure 16.3 picture sample about Yaa Gysai's *Homegoing* novel, the student instructions read:

The shapes here are "building materials" that your group may drag to the left and position to build a home "where the fire met the water" (Gyasi 300).

- *Before you use any of the building material shapes, you must discuss the question listed. (You do not need to answer all the questions, but you may only use shapes with well-pursued answers to build.)*

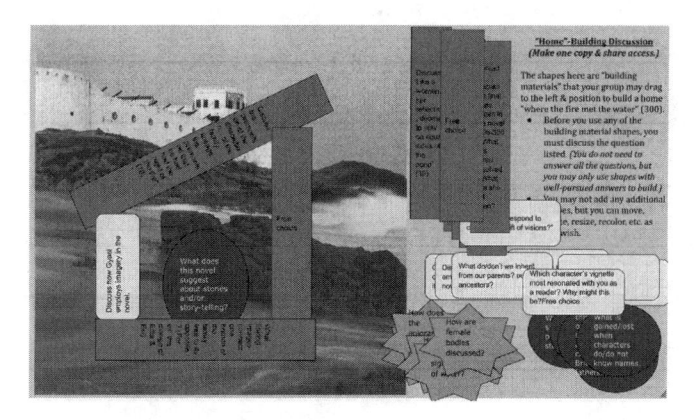

Figure 16.3 Students build a literary discussion with digital supplies.

> – *You may not add any additional shapes, but you can move, rotate,*
> *resize, recolor, etc. the shapes as you wish.*

Each digital building shape contained an analytical prompt that asked students to interpret their main topic, in this case a novel. At the conclusion of building time with partners or small groups, students can both share their digital creations and offer best-idea feedback to the rest of the class.

◆ Paper snowballs.
Similar to the colorful notecards strategy, this playful building approach prompts students to analyze a few, detailed parts of their greater topic. The snowballs are perfect for wintertime, but you could easily build a sun, pumpkin, or other items for another season. The shapes of paper could also be changed to generally (or thematically?) build paper flowers, animals, buildings, vehicles, etc. In this sample of the snowball approach, the teacher prepares by cutting out three white circles—sized large, medium, and small—for each group. Extra construction paper is also left out for student use.

DIRECTIONS: Record examples and analysis related to the bolded topics on the corresponding snowball pieces. After "stealing" snowballs from other groups, construct a cohesive "snowman" commentary.

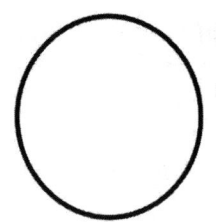

BASE: Figures of speech/poetic devices:
    • *What specific devices are employed by the poet? Consider imagery, sound color, metaphors/similes, allusions, etc. Include specific examples and discuss their effects.*

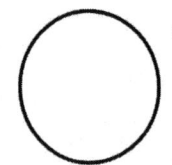

BODY: Voice/attitude/tone:
- *How would you characterize the voice of the speaker?*
- *How does the perspective / point-of-view of the poem impact its meaning?*
- *What attitude does the poet have toward the subject of the poem?*
- *Find and list examples that illustrate the tone and mood of the poem.*

HEAD: Type/structure/rhyme/meter:
- *Can this poem be classified as a specific type of poem?*
- *How does the structure used by the poet impact the poem's themes?*
- *Analyze the meter, any rhyme and/or rhyme scheme present.*

COHESIVE SNOWMAN: Significance/theme:
- *Considering all the elements noted on all your acquired snowballs, what is the significance of the message and presentation of this particular text?*

Figure 16.4 Students build a collaborative commentary by making and sharing paper snowballs.

Offer the students a set amount of time to build and a specific prompt for each piece. In the Figure 16.4 picture example, students were studying a poem by Carol Ann Duffy. Each prompt asked the learners to analyze a part of that main topic and, with additional sub questions, provide examples of how the part appeared. The groups wrote their names on the back of their circles.

After groups, use the three circles to record analysis, add a competitive, playful twist like the notecard tower building approach. Place all the base pieces together on one table, all the body pieces together on another, and all the head circles separately in another space. Then, invite the groups—one at a time as determined randomly—to review their peers' pieces and pick the most impressive base, body, and head that they can. (They cannot pick their own circles.) If five groups are playing, offer five points to the first base selected, four to the next, and so forth—tallying scores for the groups, with 15 points being a perfect score. At the end of the selecting process, celebrate the group that made the most impressive snowman parts. Then, and most importantly, prompt all the groups to synthesize (Bloom's Taxonomy level 5) their collected snowball insights into a cohesive snowman. Ask them to offer a thesis/abstract about the topic's overall significance on extras like hats, scarves, etc. with the construction paper.

Samples of Play

In this specific sample, my students had already completed reading Toni Morrion's *Sula*. They knew the content of the novel and were moving into applying their literary skills to analyze the complex text. Each student received two hexagonal cutouts—either blank or with a motif in the center of the paper. Next, learners used their books to record textual evidence and paraphrased insights about how Morrison implements the motif in the novel. After students individually accumulated analysis on their two hexagons, the class compiled all the observations into a beehive-like map.

In order for each hexagon to touch another, though, the students had to orally explain connections between the motifs. (Every time I've implemented this playful approach, the group has ultimately built an original design. No two builds are ever the same.) Once all hexagons were placed, the students and I examined the final build and reflected on which ideas appeared most centrally, which were outliers, and which appeared visually juxtaposed. Beautifully, the abstractness of Morrison's motifs became pieced together and analytically clear.

Figure 16.5 Students cover the floor with building pieces while applying their nuanced skills for effective construction.

Student-Facing Instructions

Project these instructions to incorporate this play-based approach in your secondary classroom:

1. On your hexagon, record any/all textual references and related passages to your assigned topic. Cite page numbers/resources as needed.
2. First in your groups (and later as a class), discuss connecting threads between the hexagonal topics. Use the textual evidence as a means to support connections. Place like hexagons together.
3. Use any blank hexagons to insert needed topics into your hexagonal mapping.
4. Create a singular map of _____ using the hexagonal topics provided.
5. Analyze the shape of the map as a reflection of our topic.

Application across Secondary Disciplines

Business Education	Use colorful notecards to analyze different aspects of a marketing campaign—with each color representing elements like target audience, messaging strategies, and media channels.
English Language Arts	Use the digital building approach to reinvision a novel/chapter discussion into play that examines thematic, stylistic, and/or character analysis.
Informational Technologies	Use colorful notecards to analyze the design process of engineering solutions—where each color represents stages like problem definition, brainstorming, prototyping, and evaluation.
Math	Use hexagonal cutouts to analyze geometric properties of shapes—with each hexagon representing an aspect like angles, sides, or symmetrical properties, culminating in a collaborative map.
Multilingual Language Learning	Use paper snowballs to explore thematic vocabulary sets with each circle representing a group of related words, ultimately constructing thematic word clusters.
Science	Use digital building supplies for students to discuss ecological webs—while designing one of their own using shapes and connectors.
Social Studies	Use paper snowballs to analyze the significance of a historical event—with each circle representing different figures, causes, and consequences.

References

"Higher Order Thinking: Bloom's Taxonomy – Learning Center." *UNC Learning Center*, 2024, https://learningcenter.unc.edu/tips-and-tools/higher-order-thinking/.

"How Do I Chunk Content to Increase Learning? | Center for Teaching & Learning." *UMass Amherst*, 2024, https://www.umsass.edu/ctl/resources/how-do-i/how-do-i-chunk-content-increase-learning.

17

Analytical Role-Playing and Simulations

The Physics students are used to running items down inclined planes, swinging pendulums across lab tables, and watching springs bound upward into the air. Their experiment-filled classroom is often dynamic and active. Today, though, four learners—their group members positioned behind them—exchange amused glances as they wear lanyard name-tags labeled "Force," "Mass," "Energy," and "Motion" respectively. Dramatic role-playing is a new Physics experience, but one these learners are well-prepared for, with notes sheets and after group collaboration.

"So, what would you think if I wanted to move this coffee mug off my desk?" the teacher inquires while pointing. The student named Mass leans backing, crossing her arms and scowling. Motion jumps up eagerly and wonders, "linear, rotational, or periodic?!" while Energy starts to pace the room. "I can get that started for you, sir," Force declares, flexing his arms. The other students, waiting for the pinwheel discussion to rotate, giggle, and this dynamic classroom stage—where theoretical principles come to life—accelerates to a new question.

Rationale

As discussed in the content-building section, dramatic play has been formally known as an integral component of play-based learning since the kindergarten movements of the 1900s. Positive research also pushes for role-playing remains to be encouraged within social-emotional education. Extending such

DOI: 10.4324/9781003591924-19

role-play to prompt skills application can look like simulating a decision, synthesizing resources, and inferring motivation/causation. Such active learning assists students in retaining content information and also pushes them to conceptualize, apply, and reflect on the related skills. In a 2015 study from Avondale College of Higher Education, educational experts noted that "most students [engaged in complex role-play] reported a higher passion for history… [and] commented on how the experience of gaming engaged the whole learner, visually, kinesthetically, socially and emotionally" (Kilgour et al. 2015).

How to Play

A reminder that it would never be appropriate to role-play as a marginalized person/group nor as someone whose actions/words harmed other people. This approach should not be considered if analyzing horrific, historical concepts like enslavement, genocide, fascism, etc. If unsure if your topic is appropriate to role-play, it is not. Some topics should never be made playful.

More traditionally known analytical role-playing in high school classrooms includes activities like debates and panel discussions. Personification and simulation role-playing are two additional, less-used approaches to add to teacher playbooks. Here's how to play:

Personification Role-Playing

Fellow English Language Arts (ELA) teachers will know that to personify something means to take an inanimate object and give it humanlike traits. A writer might reflect on the sun *sleeping* in the sky or the foreshadow with a knife *grinning* knowingly on the counter. Embracing personification allows secondary educators to take any class concept and ask learners to give life to that content through interpretative role-playing. To role-play using personification:

1. Place students in pairs or groups for felt safety. Then, assign each an interrelated topic from your studies. A history teacher might use different countries involved in a historical conflict, a business education teacher might use varying economic systems, or an ELA teacher might use unique characters. Sometimes I also assign one group the role of moderator. (Other times, I take on this role myself.)
2. Once students are in their groups, prompt them to review their resources about their assigned topic. They should then determine

how this topic would look if personified. Guiding questions to help this interpretation might include:

a) How does your topic interact with others? Is it friendly, antagonistic, shy, etc.?

b) What ideas does your topic quickly reject? What would this look like in a conversation?

c) To what ideas does your topic often gravitate? What would this look like in a conversation?

3. If you assigned a group the role of moderator, prompt them to instead prepare discussion questions for the topics. These might include wonderings like "who do you consider your best friends and why?" if the students are personifying countries, "what do you think the ideal life looks like" if the students are economic systems, or "what should humans most fear" if role-playing as characters. If you haven't assigned a moderator group, as a teacher prepare such questions yourself.

4. After the students have had time to prepare, engage the topics in a discussion as if they are actual people. I often use the pinwheel discussion strategy for group members to take turns conversing.

5. In the Figure 17.1 picture example, my learners personified five dramatic texts and were prompted by moderators to discuss their interpretations of the human experience. The student tearing the paper was the personification of Harold Pinter's *The Birthday Party*. As a Comedy of Menace play, she would interrupt the discussion with random actions and non-sequitur comments. The student across from her holding a pile of books was the personification of Shakespeare's *Hamlet*. As a neoclassical play, she often referenced her

Figure 17.1 Students use props and headpieces to analytically role-play as personified works of literature.

appreciation of Greek drama. The interactive of absurdist art and the Renaissance art prompted a thoughtful reflection afterwards for the entire class.

6. After the personified role-playing, prompt the learners to reflect, perhaps through writing, about the complex interconnectedness of their studied topics.

Analytical Simulations

Simulation role-playing asks learners to pretend they are engaging in a specific decision or experience from an assigned perspective. Playful Social Studies educators often prompt their students to navigate an actual historical decision as if they are the involved parties—people, roles, or nations, but the approach works wonderfully in all subject areas.

While analytical simulations often take more teacher preparation time, such initial efforts can create a multiday, playful learning opportunity for students and can follow predetermined processes like how a bill becomes a law, how to patent an idea, how to file taxes as a business, how to write a grant proposal, and so forth. The Center for Innovative Teaching and Learning at Northern Illinois University suggests additional simulations like faux marketing presentations, counseling sessions, or merchandise retailing (Northern Illinois University 2024).

Teachers can also, and perhaps more easily, ask learners to simulate being instructors or examiners themselves. An Advanced Placement or International Baccalaureate (IB) teacher, for instance, might prompt their students to participate in an essay-scoring simulation, role-playing as educators who are reading student work. After the simulation, learners can discuss what writing choices were most and least effective—and then implement these themselves.

Samples of Play

In a junior-level writing class that studies college application essays, my colleague Stephanie and I designed a simulation that asks students to "become" an admissions board at a fictitious university. First the students are assigned group-mates. As a group, they name their "just-founded" postsecondary institution and determine the key traits they'd like to find in candidates. The groups next receive a packet of application essays—each topped with a fax applicant name—as well as a scoring guide. After some time reading and considering the simulated application essays, the group members role-play an admissions decision. They discuss as an admissions board to select some applicants to admit, wait list, and deny. Finally, the groups share their ideas

Admit / Waitlist / Deny Simulation

- As a group, name your institution.
- Then, determine which three traits are most important to you in admitting candidates to your program. List these on your folded "sign."

Creative	Kind	Intelligent
Hard-working	Adaptable	Self-Starter
Innovative	Open-minded	Other?

- Next, review candidate essays and sort the applications into colored folders to represent: admit (3), waitlist (1), and deny (2)

Figure 17.2 Slideshow instructions prompt students to simulate the college admissions process in order to study effective application essays.

as a whole class and discuss which writings best reflect the strong app essay skills students have previously studied (before they then move to writing their own).

Student-Facing Instructions

Project these instructions to incorporate this play-based approach in your secondary classroom:

> Today our class will participate in an experience/simulation in which you role-play as _____. Your objective is to _____.
>
> Your preparation will look like:
>
> The actual role-playing/simulation will include:
>
> After the activity, we will reflect on our studies by considering the following:

Application across Secondary Disciplines

Business Education	Have students personify various economic systems or business models in order to discuss their strengths and weaknesses.
English Language Arts	Create a simulation in which students gather, report, edit, and publish facts about a school event as journalists.

Informational Technologies	Assign students to personify different components of a computer system (e.g., CPU, RAM, operating system) and prompt them to discuss how together they keep the system running efficiently.
Math	Prompt the students to simulate an engineering challenge that requires them to use geometrical skills.
Multilingual Language Learning	Ask the students to simulate a real-world travel scenario in which they need to use vocabulary on a specific topic (asking a local for the best tourist experience in a specific city, etc.).
Science	Assign students to personify various elements on the periodic table, describing their reactions and interactions with other elements through role-play.
Social Studies	Have students simulate the different countries involved in a historical conflict.

References

Kilgour, P., et al. Role-Playing as a Tool to Facilitate Learning, Self Reflection and Social Awareness in Teacher Education. *Int J Innov Interdiscip Res* 2(4), 8–20 (2015).

"Role Playing | Center for Innovative Teaching and Learning." *Northern Illinois University*, 2024, https://www.niu.edu/citl/resources/guides/instructional-guide/role-playing.shtml.

18

Category Challenges

The category "Makes readers uneasy" flashes on the screen, and a colorful video timer starts counting down from sixty seconds. The Creative Writing classroom fills with intense whispering, as the upperclassmen brainstorm with their table-mates at a volume inaudible to other peers.

"Narrative setting shift," quiet-shouts one student to her group mates, whose foreheads lean in nearby. "Got it!" replies the group note-taker, the self-declared fastest scribbler in the bunch.

"Many words with the 'long o' sound together—like Poe does" offers another classmate. "'Poe Os' is now written down! Like a cereal brand," the scribe giggles.

"Unfamiliar word order in the syntax!" suggests a third. "And… got it!" comes the response.

When the timer buzzes a minute later, the group has listed nine writing choices that they might, as seasoned creative composers, use to cause a reader's sense of disquietude. To the left, learners brainstormed seven and to the right, a group recorded 13 ideas.

"Remember," the scribe reassures. "The ideas need to be original ones. They won't get points for basic choices like 'scary tone.' I think we've got this round, too!"

Rationale

Bloom ranks "synthesis" as the second-highest level of critical thought (Critical Thinking and other Higher-Order Thinking Skills 2024). Put simply, this

DOI: 10.4324/9781003591924-20

level of skills-application requires students to take existing content, break it into pieces, analyze related patterns, and create new "wholes" with their knowledge. Such thinking "emphasize[s] the connections between abstract relations… rather than lists of discrete facts and procedures" (Fries et al. 2021). When students can cognitively organize ideas in these "schema" frameworks, they effectively store information, solve problems, and predict future outcomes. As a step toward full mastery of synthetic thinking, educators can provide their learners with categories and ask them to work backward to make content connections.

How to Play

Game's objective: To come up with as many correct and unique ideas for each category
Players: Two or more teams of three to four learners
Materials needed:

◆ Paper and writing utensil for each team

Setup

Preparation for category challenges is fantastically simple: brainstorm five to ten categories. The categories should prompt learners to make connections across the knowledge they've built in your course/unit. These categories work best, too, if students need to synthesize both literal (names, dates, facts, etc.) and abstract (themes, theories, concepts, etc.) ideas. For instance, if studying the United States in the 1770s, a History teacher might offer the category "Colonial Provocations." Students could offer specific events like the "Boston Tea Party" as well as concepts like "inherent natural rights."

Game Play

1. Explain the objective and tell/show the groups one category at a time.
2. Start a timer. (I often give my groups 30–60 seconds per category to brainstorm together.)
3. During the allotted time, students collaboratively list as many ideas that fit the category as possible. For instance, if seeing "Colonial

Provocations" as the category, students might list: Boston Tea Party, Boston Massacre, Taxation without Representation, Self-Government, and inherent natural rights.

4. When the timer buzzes, ask each group to read their *entire* list to the rest of the class. If another group has listed the same item as they have (like three groups named "Boston Tea Party"), the teams should cross off this idea; it is not worth points. Ideas that were unique to the round can then be tallied and each earn a point.

5. At the end of the category rounds, score the total points and declare a winner. Then, and most importantly, prompt the learners to reflect on their best answers and how course knowledge can be synthesized for advanced understanding.

Samples of Play

After our students have studied the entirety of Ray Bradbury's *Fahrenheit 451*, my sophomore-level teammates and I ask our learners to prepare an analytical project in which students explain how the novel serves as an allegory. In order to prepare the students to think about the symbolic meaning of pieces of textual evidence, we guide them with this playful category challenge game.

If you're unfamiliar with *Fahrenheit 451*, Bradbury writes about an imagined future-to-him society in which humans are obsessed with screens, books are burned in censorship, and firefighters exist as the government's authoritarian arm. My colleagues and I offer students categories like "Things Beatty Controls" and "Representations of Change" to help students review the novel's plot—Captain Beatty controls the thinking of the main character and neighbor

Fahrenheit 451 Category:

THINGS BEATTY CONTROLS

0:30

Figure 18.1 Slideshow presentation of a category and timer used as students playfully analyze *Fahrenheit 451*.

Clarisse is a catalyst of change in the protagonist's life. When synthesized with other nuances in the book, though, these categories always push students to think symbolically—noticing that Beatty controls the public's collective thoughts and how subtle references to autumn present change as well.

Student-Facing Instructions

Project these instructions to incorporate this play-based approach in your secondary classroom:

> Let's play a category challenge about _____! Work together as a team.
>
> Your game-play objective: Come up with as many original answers as you can before the time runs out.
>
> Be creative. Your team only gets points if no other team has the same, correct answer.

Application across Secondary Disciplines

Business Education	Categorize marketing techniques, such as "Product Launch Strategies" or "Market Segmentation Methods," and challenge students to list examples.
English Language Arts	Offer categories such as "Moments of Conflict" or "Impressive Authorial Language" for students brainstorm specific examples from the text.
Informational Technologies	Create categories like "Cybersecurity Threats" or "Programming Paradigms" where students brainstorm specific threats (e.g., phishing, malware) or programming concepts (e.g., object-oriented, functional) and discuss their implications.
Math	Use categories like "Real-World Applications of Algebra" or "Geometric Theorems in Architecture" to have students consider how mathematical principles apply in various contexts.
Multilingual Language Learning	Offer categories such as "Idiomatic Expressions" or "Cultural Festivals" in the target language, encouraging students to list phrases and cultural facts.

Science	Provide categories like "Cellular Processes" or "Environmental Phenomena" where students describe processes (e.g., photosynthesis, mitosis) or phenomena (e.g., climate change, earthquakes).
Social Studies	Present categories such as "Key Social Movements" and have students list movements (e.g., Civil Rights, Women's Suffrage) to analyze historical patterns

References

"Critical Thinking and other Higher-Order Thinking Skills." *Center for Excellence in Teaching and Learning*, 2024, https://cetl.uconn.edu/resources/design-your-course/teaching-and-learning-techniques/critical-thinking-and-other-higher-order-thinking-skills/.

Fries, L., et al. Practicing Connections: A Framework to Guide Instructional Design for Developing Understanding in Complex Domains. *Educ Psychol Rev* 33, 739–762 (2021). https://doi.org/10.1007/s10648-020-09561-x.

19

Reinvented Classics

When the Music Theory students open their digital Guess Who? game boards, they see the familiar white curls of Antonio Vivaldi and Wolfgang Amadeus Mozart. They're also greeted by Gustav Mahler's gaze in small glasses and Igor Stravinsky's look in looming spectacles. Over a dozen other faces and names of musical geniuses stare back at the students, too. Because they've been studying the compositional choices of these artists for months now, the advanced learners can impressively imagine the notes and tunes of each.

After their teacher explains the synthesis objectives of today's game-play, the learners are off in pairs asking thoughtful questions and "flipping" digital tiles. "Does your composer use simple structure in their compositions?" "Yes." Philip Glass and Johann Sebastian Bach surprisingly remain together. "Does your composer present harmony in a fluid, atmospheric way? "Yes." Claude Debussy remains while Ludwig van Beethoven leaves consideration. Throughout the game, the class' musical knowledge and playful natures harmonize perfectly. And when those correct guesses are finally made, each pair knows their control of music theory can definitely hit the right notes.

Rationale

Though games like Tic-Tac-Toe and Bingo can trace their roots to ancient civilizations, many of the "traditional" family games known today in the United States emerged soon after the end of World War II. With a rise in suburban

DOI: 10.4324/9781003591924-21

living and its leisure time as well as the popularization of television watching and its advertisements, 1950s American households often added classic games like "Scrabble," "Risk," and "Life" (Pruitt 2020). Providing more than mere entertainment, "playing [these] traditional board games has been shown to be related to a neural reorganization of brain areas associated with attentional control, working memory, and problem solving" (Martinez et al. 2023). Contemporary research on game-based learning in constructivist environments supports this movement of board games from the living room to the classroom: "Game-based learning also [helps] students utilize existing skills to solve problems relating to the subject matter in question… [and] process and decode essential information for understanding learning materials" (Adipat et al. 2021). To keep the prep hours low, playful teachers looking to use traditional games to support student growth needn't reinvent the spinning wheel; instead, they can modify and implement the "classics."

How to Play

In short, teachers looking to reinvent classic games most need to consider the best match in relation to their course content and objectives. Then, with digital Google Slides templates of most games free and copyable online, interested educators can simply search, modify, and share updated game boards. (Search "slide template for board games" or "slide template for [specific game name]" to find vast online treasures!) Here are some ideas on how, with a focus on playful learning, to reinvent traditional games like:

◆ *Guess Who?*

Figure 19.1 Modified *Guess Who?* digital template from Slidesmania.com; reprinted with permission.

The slide template pictured here is a creation by Paula, the impressive digital artist behind *Slidemania.com*; it is free and editable to use. *Guess Who?* is an ideal approach for learners who are synthesizing nuanced connections across texts or topics. Playful teachers can place concepts, characters, events, or figures in the board spaces. Then, students must skillfully apply their knowledge to explain these ideas to one another. As spaces are "flipped" down or stay up together, the learners are prompted to notice subtle links across the topics. For instance, in the sample picture, my International Baccalaureate (IB) English learners had first studied approximately 12 literary texts and were comparing/contrasting the authorial choices within the works. When characters were crossed off together—like Sula and Hamlet who might both be flipped over if prompted "does your character feel generationally connected to their parents?" "no" —learners connect nuances. When characters stay up together—like Gregor and Agilulf who both remain upright if asked "is your character's form something other than human?" "yes" —learners analyze parallels (Figure 19.1).

◆ Bingo

RE	V	I	E	W
		FREE SPACE		

Persuasion
Persuasive types
Ethos
Logos
Pathos
Persuasive techniques
Straw Man
Slippery Slope
Red Herring
Questioning
Repetition
Name Calling
Bandwagon
Testimonial
Plain folks
Transfer
Attention getter
Background info.
Thesis statement
Reasons
Facts
Parenthetical citations
Databases
Works Cited

Figure 19.2 Traditional Bingo board to review vocabulary words while definitions are called.

Writing -- Persuasive Mentor Text Study

PE	RS	UA	DE
FREE	PERSUASIVE PURPOSE	AGITATE AND SOLVE EXAMPLE Most affects: ☐ Logos (logic) ☐ Pathos (emotions) ☐ Ethos (credibility)	ADDRESSING OBJECTIONS EXAMPLE Most affects: ☐ Logos (logic) ☐ Pathos (emotions) ☐ Ethos (credibility)
STORYTELLING EXAMPLE Most affects: ☐ Logos (logic) ☐ Pathos (emotions) ☐ Ethos (credibility)	**FREE**	CONSISTENCY EXAMPLE Most affects: ☐ Logos (logic) ☐ Pathos (emotions) ☐ Ethos (credibility)	PROGNOSTICATE EXAMPLE Most affects: ☐ Logos (logic) ☐ Pathos (emotions) ☐ Ethos (credibility)
SOCIAL PROOF EXAMPLE Most affects: ☐ Logos (logic) ☐ Pathos (emotions) ☐ Ethos (credibility)	REASONS WHY EXAMPLE Most affects: ☐ Logos (logic) ☐ Pathos (emotions) ☐ Ethos (credibility)	**FREE**	COMPARISONS EXAMPLE Most affects: ☐ Logos (logic) ☐ Pathos (emotions) ☐ Ethos (credibility)
REPETITION EXAMPLE Most affects: ☐ Logos (logic) ☐ Pathos (emotions) ☐ Ethos (credibility)	UNIFY EXAMPLE Most affects: ☐ Logos (logic) ☐ Pathos (emotions) ☐ Ethos (credibility)	INTENDED AUDIENCE	**FREE**

Figure 19.3 A skills-focused Bingo board prompts students to apply prior knowledge about persuasive techniques.

More traditionally, the Bingo board has found its place in secondary classrooms through a format like the first picture here: with vocabulary words placed in the squares and teacher reading of the related definitions (Figure 19.2). Such playfulness works well as a content-building approach, but the Bingo board can be updated as a skills-application game, too. In the second picture, the content of earlier lessons is already preformatted into the grid. Additionally, an open space exists for examples and an evaluative selection must be made at the bottom of the square. This skills-focused approach asks the students to apply their knowledge to another reading and/or example/mentor. Learners gather textual evidence from that source, list it as examples in the grid, and—after the example collecting—the board concludes as a Bingo board for play (Figure 19.3).

- ◆ Grid/Numbered Board Games (Chutes & Ladders, Connect 4, Battleship, Jenga, rolling of dice, etc.)

Analytical discussion pushes students to consider and converse about content-related skills near the end of units. In a low-prep, playful approach,

Chutes & Ladders

100	99	98	97	96	95	94	93	92	91
81	82	83	84	85	86	87	88	89	90
80	79	78	77	76	75	74	73	72	71
61	62	63	64	65	66	67	68	69	70
60	59	58	57	56	55	54	53	52	51
41	42	43	44	45	46	47	48	49	50
40	39	38	37	36	35	34	33	32	31
21	21	23	24	25	26	27	28	29	30
20	19	18	17	16	15	14	13	12	11
1	2	3	4	5	6	7	8	9	10

Figures 19.4 A numbered grid game board that could be paired with numbered analytical questions to prompt students to apply knowledge about a novel.

teachers can pair the play of any grid-like/numbered game board with a numbered list of discussion prompts. As students playfully navigate the game board—updated with numbers as needed by the teacher, they can collaborate in their analytical thinking by reading and answering corresponding prompts (Figure 19.4). (For especially low-prep, consider first using artificial intelligence (AI) to write a set number of analytical discussion prompts for your targeted level and objectives. Then, update the AI-created draft with tweaks that best fit your learners and lessons.)

◆ Tic-Tac-Toe/Dots and Boxes

An easy, low-prep play approach is to change a hackneyed worksheet or list of questions into playful matches. For Tic-Tac-Toe games, reinvent the format from a linear list of requirements to a Tic-Tac-Toe board of options (Figure 19.5).

x^2-4x+3	$2x^2=3x-2$	x^2+4x+4
$3x^2-12x+9$	$x^2-2x-15$	$4x^2+4x+1$
x^2-9	$2x^2-4x+2$	$x^2+6x+10$

Figure 19.5 Math problems are reinvented as a playful Tic-Tac-Toe board.

To engage the entire class in Dots and Boxes, pair a projected grid board with skills-focused questions. Cut apart the complex questions and create a grab pile for students/pairs to come up and then solve. For each correct answer, the learner/pair can draw lines and claim boxes. The individual(s) with the most claimed squares at the end of the period wins.

Samples of Play

Card-Prompt Conversation

1. Sort the cards into three (3) piles: DRAMA, TERM, & EFFECT.
2. Deal one of each pile, and consider the combination that is prompted. For example:
   "In Hamlet, asides are/are not used to reveal relationships in that..."
3. With your partner(s), discuss specific scene(s) in the noted drama in response to the prompt.
4. Finally, flip (at least) one more drama card and compare/contrast another scene in relation to the prompt.

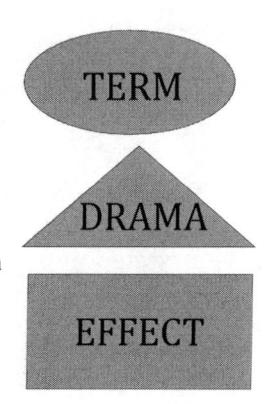

Figure 19.6 A reinvented *Dixit* game uses three draw piles to create card combinations that mimic an advanced exam.

To assist my IB seniors in preparing for a synthesis essay about the literary value of multiple texts, I have reinvented the storytelling game *Dixit*. In the traditional game, players collect cards from six different draw piles and combine the unique cards to make a creative story. In the reinvented version of the game, students select one card from three unique draw piles: one labeled "term" with a literary term listed on the inside, one labeled "text" with a studied literary work on the inside, and one labeled "effect" with a phrase from an old IB exam on the inside. The students must then successfully explain how their specific author might use or withhold the drawn literary device within the assigned work to create the described effect (Figure 19.6).

Student-Facing Instructions

Project these instructions to incorporate this play-based approach in your secondary classroom:

Let's reinvent a classic board-game order to "play" with the skills we're built! Today we will be playing a version of the game _____ in which players try to _____.

In our reinvented play, you will need to _____.

Application across Secondary Disciplines

Business Education	Reinvent *Guess Who?* to match business case studies with key strategic decisions or market trends.
English Language Arts	Transform *Dixit* into a creative writing game in which students draw cards with literary devices, characters, and themes in order to create narratives.
Informational Technologies	Adapt Bingo to include software functions or coding concepts.
Math	Transform a grid game like *Connect 4* into algebraic equation matches, where students solve equations to place their tokens.
Multilingual Language Learning	Utilize Tic-Tac-Toe with vocabulary categories and definitions in a different language.
Science	Pair *Chutes & Ladders* with a list of scientific discoveries or processes, where students must explain the significance of each step they land on.
Social Studies	Adapt *Risk* to simulate historical conflicts or geopolitical scenarios, where students analyze historical data and make strategic decisions.

References

Adipat, S., et al. Engaging Students in the Learning Process with Game-Based Learning: The Fundamental Concepts. *Int J Technol Educ (IJTE)* 4(3), 542–552 (2021). https://doi.org/10.46328/ijte.169.

Martinez, L., et al. Video Games and Board Games: Effects of Playing Practice on Cognition. *PLoS One* 18(3), e0283654 (2023). https://doi.org/10.1371/journal.pone.0283654.

Pruitt, S. "The Post World War II Boom: How America Got Into Gear." *History*, 14 May 2020, https://www.history.com/news/post-world-war-ii-boom-economy.

20

"Loose-Parts" Abstractions

It's the first day of Engineering Principles 2, but every name on her roster is already known to Mrs. Reynolds from her level-one class. One of her most beloved teacher-experiences is having repeat students. Both she and the learners can pick right up where they left off–in academic studies and in relational conversations. "In this course, we're going to study more advanced engineering concepts like thermodynamics and automation," Reynolds opens. "But first, I'd like you to consider the central concept to all those future, sophisticated designs and complex solutions: Innovation. What does it mean to drive toward 'innovation' in engineering?"

"Your first engineered prototype is to show me 'Innovation,'" she continues, "using these." Mrs. Reynolds points to her work station, which gleams with mason jars and plastic buckets of all sizes. Inside the containers students find bottle caps, rubber bands, wire scraps, foam sheets, popsicle sticks, and a dozen other assorted items. As the innovative gears turn in their minds, the students each receive a plastic plate to function as a base. Like engineers do, they begin building something new with what they already know—all while Mrs. Reynolds reflects on their content foundations through the found items.

Rationale

As discussed in the content-building "Loose Parts" section, "playing" with manipulatives greatly assists student knowledge building. In this extension of that approach, playful incorporation of assorted objects can also help learners process, represent, and decode abstract concepts more clearly.

DOI: 10.4324/9781003591924-22

In a 2015 study about epistemic visuals in science classrooms, researchers posited the need for representations of intangible theories in addition to straightforward visuals like pictures or diagrams of tangible content. Additionally, the research suggests that because

> *some visual representations need decoding, and the [people] need to learn how to read these images…, using visual representations… requires learning a new language that is specific to the medium/methods that is used (i.e., understanding an X-ray picture is different from understanding an MRI scan) and then communicating that language to other[s]*
>
> (Evagorou et al. 2015)

When students play with loose parts to visually represent abstract concepts, they both hone complex skills and formulate a creative language with which to share their advanced understandings.

How to Play

As noted in the content-building section, "loose parts" play requires the curation of small, inexpensive objects that students can manipulate into visual representations.

1. Like the content-building approach, this skills-application play begins by placing containers with loose parts in student reach.
2. Post/prompt with an abstract-thinking prompt. For example:
   a) Considering the articles we've studied, how do you personally understand the concept of "equity?"

Figure 20.1 Students use loose parts to create a diagram that examines abstract character traits.

    b) After reading this novel, what do you think the author thematically suggests about the human experience?

    c) Having studied the Renaissance, how do you define "humanism" and its conceptual impact on the world?

3. Once the prompt is shared, the students must gather loose parts and design/show their response for the abstraction. They may collaborate with partners or first work individually.

4. After a set moment of "play time," present the students with a manner in which to share their loose-parts abstractions. Options might include:

    a) Taking a photo, submitting it digitally, and writing an explanation/legend.

    b) Pair-share discussions explaining designs.

    c) Causal stand-and-deliver presentations in small groups, by volunteers, or to the whole class.

Samples of Play

One course I taught, entitled Modern World Studies, linked the humanity fields of history and literature. Students would study world events and then read the texts composed by authors of those times. At the conclusion of our World War II studies and readings, my colleagues Krista, Julie, Laura, and I prompted learners to reflect on what intangible obstacles and victories the people/writers of this era navigated. Students then created and explained loose-parts monuments to reflect their culminating knowledge of the experiences.

Student-Facing Instructions

Project these instructions to incorporate this play-based approach in your secondary classroom:

Today we will use "loose parts" (random, assorted items) to demonstrate our nuanced understandings of _____. Please use your choice assortment of loose parts to build an answer to this prompt:

Reflect on our unit studies as you create your answer. Be prepared to explain at least five specific choices you made. We'll design for _____ minutes.

Application across Secondary Disciplines

Business Education	Use pipe cleaners, pom-poms, and beads to create visual representations of business processes or organizational structures
English Language Arts	Use loose parts to symbolize key traits, motivations, or emotions of a character (not that character's physical appearance).
Informational Technologies	Utilize wooden letters, small cups, and string to construct visual models of network configurations or programming algorithms
Math	Integrate pom-poms, beads, and Lego pieces to create manipulative tools for exploring abstract mathematical concepts such as algebraic equations, geometric transformations, and statistical distributions.
Multilingual Language Learning	Use magazine cutouts, paper plates, and popsicle sticks to construct visual representations of differing grammatical conjugations and structures.
Science	Employ beads, wooden letters, and Lego pieces to build models that illustrate abstract scientific principles such as molecular structures, ecological systems, and physical forces.
Social Studies	Utilize magazine cutouts, paper plates, and string to create visual displays that depict political ideologies or societal movements.

Reference

Evagorou, M., Erduran, S. & Mäntylä, T. The Role of Visual Representations in Scientific Practices: From Conceptual Understanding and Knowledge Generation to 'Seeing' How Science Works. *Int J STEM Educ* 2, 11 (2015). https://doi.org/10.1186/s40594-015-0024-x.

21

Threading Together

The Civics students were released at the bell, but their written and webbed ideas remain—filling the classroom space like a mountain towering even after its hikers have departed. On the first table labeled "Foundations of Government" dry-erase marker scribbles offer "legislative as law-making body" and "checks/balances of power," amongst the dozens of insights. Across the room, "Marbury v. Madison," "Supreme Court" and similar sentiments encircle the "Judiciary" label. The "Federalism," "Constitution," "Elections," "Public Policy," and "Local Government" tables are all equally full of dozens of ideas erasably marked by two dozen student hands.

Glimmering beneath a note that reads "defines structure of Congress" on the "Constitution" table is a small piece of tape with vibrant threads of yarn anchored in place. The yarn stretches across the classroom to find the "Federalism" table and is again taped underneath a nearly-smudged phrase of "states' equal representation in Senate." Like a politician journeying across a nation to lobby votes, the bright string continues on to the "Elections" table, its frayed threads peeking out from a piece of tape near the three words "Electoral College system." Yarn and marked notes weave together in a vibrant, looming tapestry of tables as a testament to the students' synthesis of Civics content and a celebration of their interconnected knowledge.

Rationale

Steve Jobs, co-founder of Apple, has purportedly advised that "Creativity is just connecting things." After students have built foundational

DOI: 10.4324/9781003591924-23

content knowledge, continued learning—and inspired innovation like Job notes—occurs when they connect that knowledge with new information. Encouraging such, secondary educators can employ concept mapping as a visual tool for students to organize connected knowledge. Concept mapping involves creating diagrams that display relationships between linked concepts, typically using lines, arrows, bubbles, or hierarchies. In a biology class, for example, a concept map about photosynthesis might have "Photosynthesis" as the central node with lines branching off to linked concepts like "Sunlight," "Chlorophyll," "Carbon Dioxide," and "Oxygen." In addition to being active and engaging, this instructional approach also "has [better] long lasting effect[s] on memory [as] demonstrated in the form of better results in delayed post-test[s] as compared with other teaching/learning strategies" (Cheema and Mirza 2013). And, to be made joy-filled and playful in a secondary classroom, concept mapping simply needs the small additions of yarn and tape.

How to Play

1. After students have built an understanding of larger topics, prompt them to record nuanced ideas on a larger surface (poster paper, whiteboards, dry-erase markers on tabletops, etc.). I prefer to assign specific subcategories for these details, so that material isn't repeated across students/groups.
2. After students have recorded their ideas, ask them to review the work of others and consider a connecting prompt. Such questions might look like:
   a) What parallels can you draw between the political strategies used by different leaders in different historical eras?
   b) What common mechanisms do different biological systems use to achieve similar outcomes?
   c) How do recurring financial trends help predict future market behaviors?
3. Finally, equip learners with skeins of yarn, scissors, and tape. Ask the students to carefully navigate the room and playfully make connections that respond to the prompt. After a few minutes, the classroom looks like a spiderweb of nuanced knowledge!
4. To reflect on the play, ask students to discuss or journal their noticings. I often follow this formative assessment with a more summative one that extends the activity's connections.

Figure 21.1 Annotations about Yaa Gyasi's novel *Homegoing* fill a table, and ends of string lead to other ideas across the classroom.

(In a 2016 article I published on *Edutopia* entitled "Deep Listening Activities for Academic Discussions," I explain another playful discussion approach that includes "threading" together orally shared ideas—no tape needed.)

Samples of Play

In this sample, students had previously read seven characters' historical fiction stories from Yaa Gyasi's novel, *Homegoing*. First, the learners were assigned an individual character from the book and, using dry-erase markers on a cleanable table, they listed significant quotations and motifs within their character's chapter. Next, students navigated the seven classroom tables with yarn balls and tape dispensers. They physically threaded ideas from their character table to other related or recurring notes across the room. The classroom quite literally became a playful web of interconnected ideas. To reflect after the activity, learners wrote a formative reflection about their threaded together insights and then produced a summative project examining these ideas more thoroughly (Figure 21.2).

Figure 21.2 Threaded together ideas turn a classroom into a web of complex, student insights.

Student-Facing Instructions

Project these instructions to incorporate this play-based approach in your secondary classroom:

Let's playfully "string" together how our studies have connections "threaded" throughout. (I'm telling no "yarn"; we'll turn this room into a "web" of ideas!)

1. Write specific knowledge about the subtopic you've been assigned. Cite previously studied resources whenever possible and write clearly, so classmates can understand your ideas.
2. Navigate the classroom to read insights from your peers.
3. Consider the question:
4. Use yarn and tape to physically connect ideas in response to the prompting question.
5. Reflect on how nuances in the topic of _____ connect together.

Application across Secondary Disciplines

Business Education	Map out financial trends and use yarn to connect patterns across economic periods or market behaviors.
English Language Arts	Chart characters, motifs, and symbols in a novel and use yarn to link their impacts on a central theme.
Informational Technologies	Outline technological advancements and use yarn to connect the innovations with their historical contexts and subsequent developments.
Math	Create nodes for mathematical theorems and use yarn to connect underlying principles and applications.
Multilingual Language Learning	Chart verb conjugations, grammar rules, and thematic vocabulary groups in Spanish and then use yarn to connect to specific cultural contexts.
Science	Illustrate chemical processes and use yarn to link common outcomes.
Social Studies	Map significant historical events and use yarn to connect causes, effects, and recurring themes.

Reference

Cheema, A. & Mirza, M. Effect of Concept Mapping on Students. *Acad Achiev* 7, 125–132 (2013).

22

Bracket Battles

All pairs of students' eyes in the IB Math: Applications & Interpretations class stare at the same shared dataset. A listing of months dominates the left-hand side of the table and numbers measuring sales, units, production costs, and market demand indexes fill the other columns. These learners are near-ready for their college-credit exams, though; they're skillful in analyzing data and confident about articulating insights.

When the class' five minutes of reading time ends, Mr. Addison holds a large plastic trophy donned with past student names. "For the victors to sign," he announces, as he adds a tournament bracket visual to the projector screen. "You and your partner will compose a single sentence with some insight about the data. We'll then face off in bracket battles to find who has the most correct, concise, and interesting analysis."

Pencils, calculators, and minds race. Mathematical ideas fill poster paper. When the time's up, the first-round posters are arranged side-by-side: "The maximum profit point at $250,000 has a constraint of 30 production units…" versus "The regression analysis forecasts a 15% increase in sales over…" Student competitors hold their breath as peers consider and vote.

"Round Two!" Mr. Addition directs—and the class continues to calculate whose math will be the top contender and "bracket" the competition.

DOI: 10.4324/9781003591924-24

Rationale

Now an infamous staple in the March Madness NCAA Tournament, competitive brackets actually originated in an 1851 chess competition run by Howard Stauton, also the creator of the modern chessboard. In his single-elimination bracket setup, Staunton intended to find "the two best players in… a collision for the chief prize" (Guerrieri 2021). Secondary educators also strive for the best work from their learners. Pushes to include more collaborative learning activities also have some teachers implementing peer assessments more often, in hopes that learners will propel one another to such better success.

The reality, though, is that peer review only works well sometimes—when proper instruction moves students away from simple affirmations of "good job" and when clear, repeated examples model for learners what best work indeed looks like. Recent research about postsecondary medical school students found, in fact, that peer-reviewers needed multiple opportunities to review effective models in order to articulate helpful feedback. According to the study, learners need clear samples and recurring peer assessments for

Figure 22.1 A plastic trophy serves as the prize after advanced learners playfully participate in a bracket battle with competing thesis statements.

effective results. When implemented properly, though, peer assessment can "increase [students'] analytical skills as well as their ability to achieve their learning objectives and fulfill tasks related to the analysis of problems" (Lerchenfeldt et al. 2019).

This playful "bracket battle" approach incorporates a beyond-chess bracket setup to expose students to strong examples again and again—while also affording learners those repeated opportunities to successfully review best peer work (Figure 22.1).

How to Play

1. Prompt learners, likely in pairs, to complete a skills-application task related to your area of study. For example, students could be prompted to write an effective DBQ thesis, a precise scientific abstract, a thorough mathematical proof, a strong literary claim, etc.

2. Ask students to show their completed task in a clear, visual way. If asked to write some of the academic sentences noted above, for instance, they could write these in large print on a piece of poster paper.

3. Find/create a bracket board and place pairs within it. I prefer to use an online randomizer to assign numbered positions to students.

4. For the "Battle," move through the brackets and hear both competing submissions. When conducting this playful approach in my own classroom, I usually read the student samples to allow the students to separate publicly from their submissions. Use the visuals to show the two competing ideas side by side.

5. With each pairing, ask the class (but not the competitors for that round) to vote for the sample they find to be more effective. Mentimeter, an interactive presentation website, has a "vote" feature that teachers can easily clear/reuse after each round and that hides the total number of votes cast for each competitor—ensuring that students don't know if one submission received no votes (Figure 22.2) (Mentimeter 2024).

6. Repeat the bracket competition until two finalists and then one victor remains. This playful approach means that learners receive repeated peer-assessment exposure to the class' best work.

7. At the end of the game, use the final submission(s) as student models as your learners continue to refine their advanced studies.

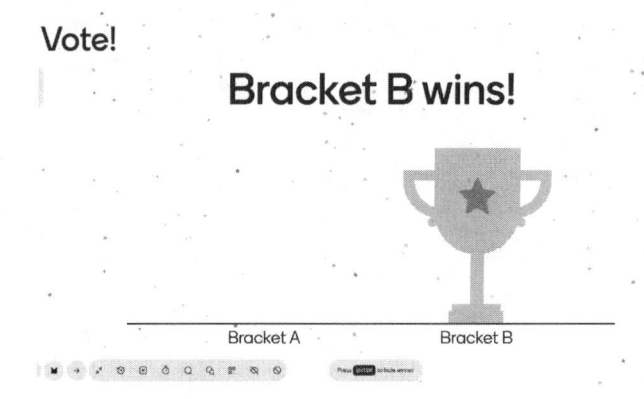

Figure 22.2 Mentimeter.com can tally votes and offer a total-free visual of which students move on to the next round.

Samples of Play

In my college-credit IB course, seniors compose practice exam thesis statements and then "bracket battle" to find the class' strongest. I like to run this approach in March to align with the NCAA tournament, and I playfully award my winning students with a small, plastic trophy. Most importantly, the peer models that emerge from this game serve as our whiteboard posted samples for the rest of the school year as learners continue to assess and refine what strong writing they can bring to their IB exams.

Student-Facing Instructions

Project these instructions to incorporate this play-based approach in your secondary classroom:

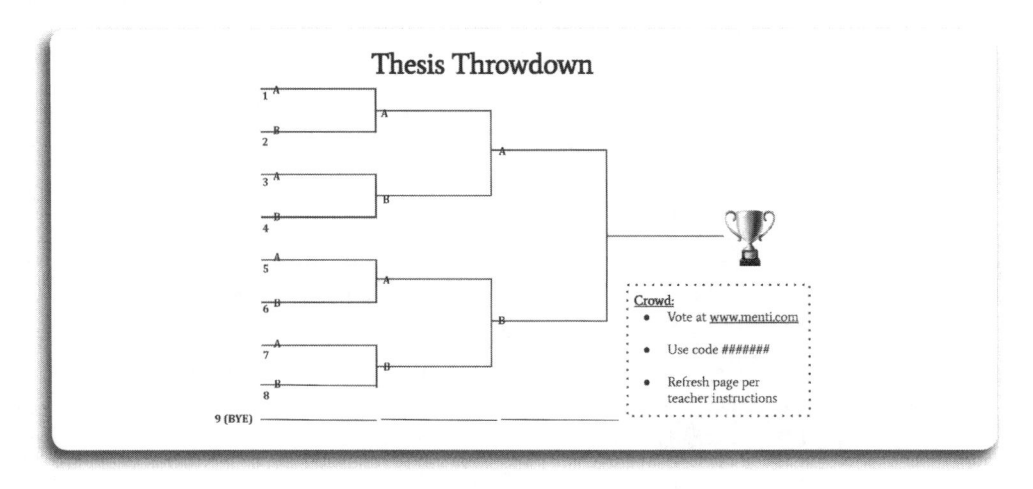

Application across Secondary Disciplines

Business Education	Prompt students to present marketing pitches within a bracket battle.
English Language Arts	Prompt creative writing students to present three sentences of powerful imagery within a bracket battle.
Informational Technologies	Prompt students to present innovative tech solutions within a bracket battle.
Math	Prompt students to present proof solutions in a visual format within a bracket battle.
Multilingual Language Learning	Prompt students to present learned-language dialogue within a bracket battle to find the most fluent and accurate work speaking.
Science	Prompt students to present scientific posters within a bracket battle.
Social Studies	Prompt students to present historically analytical thesis statements within a bracket battle.

References

Guerrieri, V. "A Brief History of the March Madness Sports Tournament Bracket." *Mental Floss*, 12 March 2021, https://www.mentalfloss.com/article/643661/march-madness-sports-tournament-bracket-history.

Lerchenfeldt, S., Mi, M. & Eng, M. The Utilization of Peer Feedback During Collaborative Learning in Undergraduate Medical Education: A Systematic Review. *BMC Med Educ* 19, 321 (2019). https://doi.org/10.1186/s12909-019-1755-z.

Mentimeter. 2024, https://www.mentimeter.com/app/home.

23

Playing with Skills—Via AI Support

Every high school teacher—perhaps especially those in the math field—have heard that ever-frustrating question: 'When are we ever going to use this in the future?' Before their final course exam, the Geometry students of room 212 are role-playing that experience as a culmination of their studies. Chromebooks open and ChatGPT approved, the learners use a standard prompt to instruct AI to take the role of a geometry-skeptical student. In a race against one another and the classroom clock, they'll tell the program all the real-world applications Geometry can hold—until hopefully earning a winner's bell "I got it!" response.

The timer begins and the fingers fly.

"Imagine you're rearranging your room..." one student begins.

"You know those 3D figures that make up your favorite video games..." writes another.

"Isn't rearranging my room just moving stuff around?" and "how exactly does geometry help in making 3D figures for video games?" the AI quips back. The classroom seems to collectively sigh. They're going to have to be more acute in their specifications...

Rationale

Artificial intelligence (AI) is being discussed more and more as an adaptive teaching assistant for educators who are overtasked and short on time.

DOI: 10.4324/9781003591924-25

Currently, AI platforms can grade essays, congregate data, create simple instructions, design presentations, and—in the time that this manuscript takes to be published—will likely tackle more complex tasks by the day. In addition to being a responsive teacher's aid and effective content tutor, AI can serve as the best partner we'd want to join our students in advanced play. Because they "explicitly aim to act as agents in the classroom environment by adaptively tapping into students' learning process," AI partners can responsively ask students to apply their skills in always-new game scenarios (Kim et al. 2022). As the quotation attributed to George Couros predicts, "Technology will not replace great teachers but technology in the hands of great teachers can be transformational." Here's how to use AI to playfully build skills-application practices in your high school classroom:

How to Play

*** *Please note: I am composing this guide in the summer of 2024 and currently "playing" with ChatGPT 4. As technology quickly advances, the specificity of my ideas will also quickly become outdated. Regardless, this playful approach can be modified to best fit with the AI you, dear reader, have access to while reading.*

Before play: Connect with your IT department to discuss student access to AI platforms. Your students might have limited access on school devices and/or Wi-Fi and proactive steps can ensure your playful activity works when you want it to.

"Playing" with AI in this approach looks similar to the "Analytical Role-Playing and Simulation" approach. Instead of students working together, though, here they partner with AI. Learners can take either part in the role-playing: being the expert responder as AI asks questions or being the content-applying questioner as AI role-plays for responses.

Use this general prompt with your students or model after the content-specific one:

◆ General prompt (AI questions and student responds):

Imagine you are a freshman in high school who has just finished studying _____ but doesn't fully understand the importance. You will ask a series of questions to better appreciate the topic. As the AI, you will role-play as the student and ask questions. I, as the educator, will provide responses based on my knowledge. If my questions help you understand the topic's importance, indicate when you "get" the significance. Ready to ask questions now?

◆ Content-specific prompt (student questions and AI responds):

I am a delegate at the Constitutional Convention of 1787. AI, as George Washington, you are leading discussions on the structure of the new government. You have differing opinions from other delegates—individuals like Alexander Hamilton and Thomas Jefferson—about the balance of power between states and the federal government. Prepare to articulate your vision for the future of the United States, considering the challenges of the Articles of Confederation and the need for a stronger central authority. I will ask you questions about executive power, legislative representation, and the role of the judiciary in ensuring a balanced government. Understand, Mr. Washington? If so, we can begin.

To add a competitive twist to the play, consider making students race to the AI's "I get it!" response if using the general prompt. If using the content-specific prompt, be sure to have students assess the credibility of the AI answers after play. We want to ensure that students know that responsible AI users check for bias, accuracy, and completeness each use.

Samples of Play

For this example, I used the general prompt above and pretended to be studying the play *Hamlet* by William Shakespeare. I inputted the text—with topic added—exactly into ChatGPT, and it responded as the student. My responses follow in the gray boxes (Figure 23.1).

I have not included the entire discourse but ultimately—after perhaps six or so minutes of offering analysis about the play—I was able to move my reluctant AI "student" to tell me:

I get it! Hamlet's journey is about grappling with his own doubts, his relationships, and his place in the world. It's not just about revenge; it's about his internal struggles and how he learns to navigate them, even if it leads to a tragic end. Thanks for helping me understand it better!

Student: I just finished reading *Hamlet*, but I'm still a bit confused. Why is this play considered such a big deal in literature? What makes *Hamlet* more important than other stories?

It's a timeless tale about indecision and mortality.

Student: Okay, that makes sense, but what exactly is Hamlet indecisive about? And why does that indecision matter so much in the story?

Hamlet is indecisive about whether or not to seek the revenge the ghost prompts. He is unsure about whether killing his uncle would be moral. It matters because we all wonder at times if what we are going is honorable. And within a divine plan.

Student: Oh, so Hamlet's struggle is about figuring out what's right and wrong. But why does his indecision take up so much of the play? Couldn't he just decide and move on? What's the bigger message here?

↓

Figure 23.1 ChatGPT's OpenAI.

Student-Facing Instructions

Project these instructions to incorporate this play-based approach in your secondary classroom:

Today, we will apply the skills you've developed about _____ _____ to engage in a role-play activity with Artificial Intelligence (AI). You will play the role of student/teacher, and AI will play the role of

_____.

Your objective is to:

After we play, we'll assess your knowledge and how well AI seemed to understand the content.

Remember: Responsible users of AI need to always check for bias, completeness, and accuracy. The AI is only pretending—like us in this role-play; it is using open sources online to role-play as best as it can, but it is not perfect.

Application across Secondary Disciplines

Business Education	Prompt learners to interact with AI to explore economic theories—with AI role-playing as an economist discussing forecasting trends.
English Language Arts	Prompt learners to role-play as critics debating a novel's interpretations with AI through specific literary lenses.

Informational Technologies	Prompt students to role-play debugging sessions with AI—where they provide code snippets and AI responds with troubleshooting guidance.
Math	Prompt students to pose complex problems to the AI as it responds with step-by-step solutions.
Multilingual Language Learning	Prompt AI to hold conversations with students in a foreign language, allowing learners to practice vocabulary and grammar in a role-played context.
Science	Prompt learners to role-play as scientists discussing a controversial hypothesis with the AI, and it takes the role of a skeptical peer-reviewer.
Social Studies	Extend the Constitutional Convention example—with students role-playing with different historical figures like Benjamin Franklin or James Madison; then ask them to compare/evaluate responses.

Reference

Kim, J., Lee, H. & Cho, Y. H. Learning Design to Support Student-AI Collaboration: Perspectives of Leading Teachers for AI in Education. *Educ Inf Technol* 27, 6069–6104 (2022). https://doi.org/10.1007/s10639-021-10831-6.

Section III

Play-Based Assessments

Using play to assess learners is an emerging and therefore still understudied topic. Even in application at the primary education level, "play-based pedagogy calls for additional scholarship in both assessment theory and practice" (DeLuca 2018). Researchers note that the largest, current play-based assessment (PBA) obstacle is limited teacher access to training and resources. Hopefully this collection of both—and other emerging sites and publications—can assist playfully minded educators.

We do know, though, that play-based assessments take place in more real-world "naturalistic environment[s]… whereas traditional standardized development tests require specific response to examiner-provided stimulus" (O'Grady and Dusing 2015). While showing skills through play, learners can demonstrate their ability to perform only the learned skills—not their ability to additionally master standardized exam wordings and structures. Play-based assessments are "child-driven rather than examiner-driven" and need to find their places in secondary schools (O'Grady and Dusing 2015).

In my current studies, I have found published trainings and documents to assist play-based assessment in grades K-4, but little guidance for secondary levels. As effective educators do, though, we can consider and scaffold the resources that exist. In elementary grade play-based assessments, educators design opportunities like the role-playing, card prompting, and simulations noted in early sections. They make the learning objectives known to learners and observable to teachers by using clear, categorized checklists as summative assessments. Additionally, educators assessing with play in primary classrooms allow students to share their metacognitive processes through prompting questions. (It's worth noting that state learning standards for the secondary level are including more language about learner metacognition, too.) All these strategies can be implemented for the benefit of older learners as well.

Here is a low-prep, play-based assessment approach to try in your secondary classroom.

References

DeLuca, C. "Play-Based Learning: Assessment." *Encyclopedia on Early Childhood Development*, Université de Montréal, 1 February 2018.

O'Grady, Michael G. & Dusing, Stacey C. Reliability and Validity of Play-Based Assessments of Motor and Cognitive Skills for Infants and Young Children: A Systematic Review. *Phys Ther* 95(1), 25–38 (2015). https://doi.org/10.2522/ptj.20140111.

24

Role-Playing/Simulation Assessments

Semester's end is always the tastiest time in Advanced Culinary Arts class. Principal Bella enters the kitchen classroom to find three other visiting staff members, a beautifully set table, and a class menu of lunch options. She's a vegetarian, so politely requests a sample of the described "elegant yet indulgent" Mushroom Wellington. When the student chef—doubling now as a waiter—brings a golden, flaky puff-pastry speckled with a light drizzle of balsamic glaze, Bella knows she's made the perfect selection. The young cook explains his choice to pair spinach, mushrooms, and leeks with parsley, sage, and tarragon. He describes his preparation of a brunoise of shallots and garlic. He outlines his thinking about sautéeing the filling. And, all the while, Principal Bella enjoys every delicious bite of well-seasoned learning.

When Bella, with a full stomach and thankful heart, stands to return to her office, she sees the culinary teacher conferring with the student chef at a side table. Together the two read and reflect on assessment checklist items like "plates dish attractively with attention to garnish and/or sauce details" and "understands flavor balance to create a dish with complementing herbs and aromatics." She and the learner deem him proficient in the categories, but evidence of how skills are always growing comes next in the discussion: The learner explains how initially the puff pastry was too sticky, so he remembered their binding ingredient studies and tried adding a small amount of breadcrumbs to the mixture. The culinary teacher praises his learning.

Bella, quietly walking away, feels impressed to have found this additional taste of learning—even within a summative assessment.

DOI: 10.4324/9781003591924-27

Rationale

Using role-playing and simulations as play-based assessments allows educators to not only assess student skills but also assess student skills within a *real-world scenario*. Such assessments change the summative process from being about an earned score to being about feedback that identifies strengths and areas for improvement in practical contexts. Sometimes used in healthcare education, for example, a patient-caregiver simulation might ask learners to demonstrate their clinical skills in a controlled, relevant environment. Additionally, students do not exit the simulation assessment with only a static exam percentage; instead, they receive standards-focused feedback through a checklist rubric and instructor observations. Especially unique to such play-based assessments, research also suggests that "student participants learned as they engaged in these scenario-based simulations"—even when in the assessment form (Battista 2017). (I'm not sure when students complete traditional exams like multiple-choice or short-essay ones, they'd report having *continued learning* during that experience!) While role-playing and simulation assessments can be more time- and resource-heavy, they can also shift our thinking about assessment and its feedback to best support learners.

Sample of Play

One of my current courses—a professional writing class for high school juniors—contains an interview skills unit. Throughout our instruction of interview skills, my colleagues and I have evolved our summative assessment of learners' understandings from a more traditional exam model to a role-playing simulation. In the simulation, students consider a dream job and locate an actual employer of this position. They then simulate interview preparation in which they research the employer, anticipate interview questions, and practice responses.

The interview unit ultimately concludes with students "arriving" at an assigned time for their interview and we teachers role-playing as their potential employers. (Classmates in the classroom are beginning the next unit with self-paced directions.) During the assessment, learners are scored using a simulation checklist that measures if they arrived on time, waited professionally in the mock waiting area, offered anecdotes in their interview, spoke clearly, followed up with a thank you email, and so forth.

Additionally, students record their interview assessments, listen to themselves afterward, and reflect on their successes and areas for further growth. As the research on role-playing assessments purports, the summative experience engages learners, offers them real-world experience, and results in individualized feedback.

Sample Rubric

This secondary-level rubric extract modifies a sample, primary-level "play skills checklist" that was initially studied and created by Dr. Bruce Baker and Dr. Alan Brightman (Baker and Brightman 2024).

	Does Not Do (1)	Does with Much Help (2)	Does with Some Help (3)	Does Alone (4)
Category A: Interview Preparation				
Learns at least ten (10) facts about the employer				
Lists at least five anticipated interview questions related to the job/field				
Outlines at least five planned interview responses related to anticipated questions				
Category B: Interview Nonverbals				
Arrives to the waiting area ten minutes before the assigned time				
Sits pleasantly and patiently in the waiting area				
Professionally engages with interviewer using learned nonverbal skills (strong posture, eye contact, etc.)				

Student-Facing Instructions

Project these instructions to incorporate this play-based approach in your secondary classroom:

Let's show your skills through a simulated assessment!

This unit, you've been learning to _____. In order to show your understanding, we will conclude this unit with a mock _____.

In this simulation, your learning objectives are to:

Application across Secondary Disciplines

Business Education	Assess while students simulate a business pitch to potential investors that requires them to prepare financial statements and a business plan.
English Language Arts	Assess while students take on the roles of characters from a novel during a mock trial, defending their actions using textual evidence.
Informational Technologies	Assess while students role-play as IT support staff, resolving simulated technical issues.
Math	Assess while students act as financial advisors, using mathematical models to give investment advice to mock clients.
Multilingual Language Learning	Assess while students participate in a simulated cultural exchange.
Science	Assess while students simulate a scientific conference, presenting post-lab research findings.
Social Studies	Assess while students reenact historical events or debates as key figures.

References

Baker, Bruce L. & Brightman, Alan J. "Play skills checklist." Brookes, Brookes Publishing, 2024, https://brookespublishing.com/resource-library/play-skills-checklist/.

Battista, A. An Activity Theory Perspective of How Scenario-Based Simulations Support Learning: A Descriptive Analysis. *Adv Simul* 2, 23 (2017). https://doi.org/10.1186/s41077-017-0055-0.

25

Final Thoughts

As lifelong learning educators do during the summer months, I've brought my laptop to various kid lessons and activities in June, July, and August while working on this manuscript. I've researched and written on park benches as my children take morning golf lessons. I've considered and composed in a steamy balcony as my daughter learns to swim below. I've reread and revised at a high-top table inside a skatepark as my son navigates ramps and tricks on his board. These playful moments have not only allowed me to stay focused on this work but also provided confirmation: play is the way in which children most naturally engage and grow.

Play and secondary education need not be strangers. And, while playful lessons will likely not dominate every day of instruction in your advanced courses, causal integration of play can naturally remedy the apathy creeping into high school classrooms. As play remains constant throughout childhood across generations, let's strive to also maintain its educational presence—despite any trending waves and emerging technologies.

As you journey beyond this book, I hope you find opportunities to blend your existing instruction with playful approaches. May this resource inspire you to create learning moments through seeming silliness, encourage you to continue growing as an educator, and remind you—as writing it has me—that "playing around" with our knowledge is a continuous and ever-evolving adventure.

DOI: 10.4324/9781003591924-28

26

Special Thanks

My two decades as an educator have been greatly influenced—both professionally and personally—by incredible people. Because my PLC teams are highly collaborative and full of wonderfully intelligent women, the playful ideas presented here grew from conversations with those inspiring colleagues. Specifically, I offer much influence and appreciation to my IB teammate and department head Vicki Quinn, my Literary Analysis partners Krista Dolan, Sarah Meyer, Brooke Mraz, and Tepa Yang as well as my consistent College and Career Writing teammates Hannah Agyekum, Kathy Krause, and Stephanie Rodgers. Furthermore, my school's entire ELA department has been one that shares effective approaches and challenges our own status quo. I'm also thankful for colleagues and leaders that consistently measure efforts by what's best for students—especially my career-long principal, Mike Frieder, for trusting his staff to try new approaches and to make learner-centered decisions.

Personally, my teaching and writing endeavors were first inspired by my own playful educators in the Howards Grove School District: Mrs. Wesener who encouraged through pop-up books and Mrs. Reyer who entertained with silly voices. My parents, Wayne and Leah Heusterberg, have always offered me love, support, and best examples. My husband, Lucas—my "favorite big person"—cheers me on in all endeavors ceaselessly and my two children, Cael and Evelyn, have patiently allowed our summer mornings to begin with cold brew coffee and mom book-writing time. Those three bring me joy and make me proud—beyond words.

DOI: 10.4324/9781003591924-29

Printed in the United States
by Baker & Taylor Publisher Services